A HISTORY OF SRINIKETAN

The Padma Boat or the houseboat (afloat on River Padma) aboard which Rabindranath Tagore did much of his writing; it was while travelling by this family-houseboat that he interacted with the rural populace of Selidaha for the first time

A HISTORY OF SRINIKETAN

Rabindranath Tagore's Pioneering Work in Rural Reconstruction

UMA DAS GUPTA

PAPER MISSILE
NIYOGI BOOKS

Published by
NIYOGI BOOKS
Block D, Building No. 77,
Okhla Industrial Area, Phase-I,
New Delhi-110 020, INDIA
Tel: 91-11-26816301, 26818960
Email: niyogibooks@gmail.com
Website: www.niyogibooksindia.com

Editor: Arunima Ghosh
Design: Shashi Bhushan Prasad
Cover Design: Trisha De Niyogi

ISBN: 978-93-91125-44-8
Publication: 2022
Reprint: 2025

Printed at: Niyogi Offset Pvt. Ltd., New Delhi, India

Dedicated to the memory of my parents
S.C. Ray and Sati Ray
who were among the pioneers of
the Sriniketan work

‘Here is thy footstool and there rest thy feet where live the poorest, and lowliest, and lost.’

—Rabindranath Tagore,
Gitanjali (Song Offerings), 1913

‘Once I lived in a boat on the Padma and devoted myself to literature. I then used to fancy that my only vocation was to delve with the pen deep in the mine of ideas, that I was not competent for any other work. But I failed to persuade anybody that the real field of home rule was in the village and that the cultivation of the field must start at once. And so for a while I set aside my pen and decided that I should myself undertake the work.’

—Rabindranath Tagore,
Letters from Russia, 1931

‘Of course, turning out songs is my proper work. But those who are unfortunate cannot afford to limit their choice to the works they can do.’

—Rabindranath Tagore,
On Constructive Work—A Letter, 1921

CONTENTS

INTRODUCTION

> Tagore had warned the world that it was headed along a dangerous and destructive path and we now know that he was right. He spoke about an alternative course, and carried out such practical experiments as his resources allowed, in the hope that they would set an example, which would be followed. We have seen a century of economic exploitation and conflict, and the only hope may lie in turning to Tagore's path based on social cooperation, but people today do not face the future optimistically. Blind habits, coercion, denial and destruction, and despair, get in the way of positive change. Listening to Tagore could at least revive his faith in humanity and give us hope and courage.[1]

It would not be fair to think of Rabindranath Tagore's experiments in rural reconstruction as ideas and targets only to obtain the economic development of villages. Though economic development was a very important goal in the Sriniketan work, there was the 'other' no less important goal of bringing joy to the lives of the village people. He knew intuitively that poverty was not the only problem; unhappiness was also a problem. If we think over those words, we cannot miss the feeling and conviction with which he said in a speech to the Visva-Bharati Sammilani (Association) in Calcutta in 1922,

> It is hard to imagine a life as cheerless as in our rural areas. I could see no way out. It is far from easy to do something for people who have cultivated weakness for centuries and do not know what self-help is. Still I had to make a start. At one time our villages were in intimate contact with the manifold culture of India. They were cherished and served by all capable persons with the best that their minds produced. Today the villages are fatally neglected. They are fast degenerating into serfdom, compelled to offer to the ungrateful towns cheerless and unintelligent labour for work carried on in an unhealthy and impoverished environment. The object of the Institute is to bring back life in its completeness to the villages, making them self-reliant and self-respectful, acquainted with the cultural tradition of their own country and competent to make efficient use of the modern resources for the improvement of their physical, intellectual and economic condition.[2]

Rabindranath's work for rural reconstruction was a remarkable combination of a poet's faith in humanity along with a reformer's zeal. Anyone who knows anything of the Sriniketan work cannot miss that remarkable combination. Anyone who knows anything about Rabindranath would know him as a poet of joy, a poet who danced with his students, who wrote plays and acted in them, who invited dancers from other parts of the country to his Santiniketan school, who wanted Sriniketan to bring music and cheer to the villager's life. He was a poet and a singer who lived in action. There is a charming Abanindranath 'Watercolour' of Rabindranath as a dancing *baul* holding up the *ektara* on his head just as the *baul*s do when they sing and dance. Rabindranath created the role of a blind *baul* in his play *Falguni* and acted that role himself, when *Falguni* was staged. His life and work as an actor, singer, playwright, and reformer, were combined to create and foster an alternative education for bringing life in its completeness to society, whether it be in the village work at Sriniketan or at his school for children in Santiniketan.

It is widely discussed among aficionados how even Rabindranath's melancholy songs can turn magically sublime in transcending sadness and in transcending the negative. It was perhaps for this ethereal quality that an argumentative section among the Bengali intelligentsia were sometimes angry with him. For example, a group of budding Bengali poets of the 1950s compared him unfavourably with Baudelaire. They complained that while Baudelaire's poetry highlighted the existence of 'evil', Rabindranath's poetry did not. They criticized Rabindranath for what they regarded as his indifference to evil. He faced many such criticisms. His own social milieu hardly understood what he was trying to do. About this sad fact, his son Rathindranath, or Rathi (1888–1961, a graduate in agriculture from the University of Illinois at Urbana, first Joint Secretary of Visva-Bharati, gave his lifelong services to his father's institution), wrote thus in his memoirs, *On the Edges of Time*,

> I think few writers have had to face such severe and unfair criticism as Father during the greater part of his life. Hardly any of these were literary criticisms—they were acrimonious and sometimes even scurrilous. One obvious reason for the persistence of such vituperations appearing regularly in a section of the Bengali press, was that the editors had early discovered that slandering Father paid handsomely.[3]

Rabindranath referred to his rural work as his 'life's work'[4]. This study here on Sriniketan's history intends to document the work of rural reconstruction and examine its pioneering features of integrated thought and action. The idea, as we have read above, was premised on a unique proposition of 'bringing life in its completeness' to the Indian village through the Santiniketan-Sriniketan alternative education. This education was created on the founder's radical ideas of bringing the city and the village close, by giving elementary instruction in the sciences to the students and combining it with their practical work at grassroots, training them to think about the environment by observing it for themselves. They were expected to describe and record the knowledge they acquired and to 'connect' what they observed with their everyday life. Another unique aspect of this alternative education was including awareness and training in art and craft as a part and parcel of the students' everyday lives. Innovative design of everyday things was included in Santiniketan-Sriniketan's art and craft syllabus. The creation of beauty was given an important place in Rabindranath's ideas of an alternative education.

Global industrialization had left the Indian rural communities muddled and clueless about their future. It was a time when England and Europe were making rapid progress in developing industrial technology. That movement was reflected in India's colonial government's policies. Rabindranath and Gandhi were not in favour of the urban industrial society to which the colonial rulers were inclined. They saw India's salvation in rural India where the majority of the population lived. Both Rabindranath and Gandhi set out on the path of rejuvenation through an alternative education, which gave priority to rural reconstruction, Gandhi in his ashrams and Rabindranath at his Santiniketan-Sriniketan institutions. Rabindranath wrote that his goal was to adapt 'modern methods of education in a truly Indian cultural environment'[5].

The rural work at Sriniketan spearheaded a movement to integrate art and craft with everyday life experiences by reviving the traditional crafts and reviving them with new and creative designs. Santiniketan and Sriniketan created a novel and sophisticated taste for these newly-designed traditional crafts among India's cultured elite. The Santiniketan design came to be loved. We shall see in the chapters that follow how every student in Sriniketan's scheme of a multi-layered education was compulsorily apprenticed to learn at least one traditional craft along with their chosen programmes of other vocational courses.

Rabinbranath brought together various strands of universalist thought and influence when setting up his radical university, named Visva-Bharati, at Santiniketan-Sriniketan. This institution developed an integrated and holistic system of education from the primary school stage to the university level, in which histories and cultures, art and craft, and the agricultural sciences played a key role. Visva-Bharati's student population came both from the cities and the villages. Some students and teachers also came from the West, as Visva-Bharati was India's first 'international university'. The teachers and students lived as a closely-knit and nature-loving community. They studied and painted in open air classes. They were not burdened with the colonial syllabus. The painter, Nandalal Bose (1882–1966), took charge of Santiniketan's art school, Kala-Bhavana, and became its first principal in 1922. He and his teacher, Abanindranath Tagore (1871–1951, founder of the Bengal School of Art and Rabindranath's nephew), were at the forefront of the nationalist rebellion against 'academic' art. But the rebellion was not narrow-minded. It's intention was for a synthesis of the East and the West, by bringing some new ideas and actions into the art and craft education at Santiniketan and Sriniketan.

In practical ways and in principles, the synthesis was made of various influences. One of the early influences was from Santiniketan's association with a group of creative thinkers from Asia, who were spearheading a Pan-Asian Movement that questioned Western hegemony in art and artistic expression. A pioneer of the Pan-Asian Movement was Kakuzo Okakura (1863–1913, Japanese scholar and author of *The Book of Tea*). He came to Calcutta in 1904, when he met Rabindranath, and they became friends. Okakura admired and supported Rabindranath's Santiniketan school.[6] Nandalal's Kala-Bhavana syllabus included Okakura's artistic principles of giving importance to nature, tradition, and creativity, which were the same as Rabindranath's artistic principles.[7]

Another important influence on the art and culture of Santiniketan-Sriniketan in the 1920s came via Europe. At the time, Rabindranath was a famous international figure as the first non-European Nobel Laureate and his reputation was particularly strong in Germany and Austria. He was also, at the time, travelling widely in the world to reach out and spread the word about his Visva-Bharati International University, which he was setting up at Santiniketan as a centre for a fellowship of minds from the East and the West. He was giving his lectures to many audiences in Japan, Europe, America, and Asia, with an open invitation to those who empathized with his idea of a meeting place to learn about each other's histories and cultures and try to gain an understanding of oneself and others. One of those who responded to Rabindranath's invitation was a very young Austrian art historian, Stella Kramrisch (1896–1993, Czech art historian, a celebrated specialist on Indian art), who was at the time engaged in her doctoral work in London on the subject of early Buddhist sculpture in India. She came to Santiniketan in 1922 on Rabindranath's invitation to teach Western art history at Kala-Bhavana and also to continue with her research on Buddhist art in India. Trained in European art history at Vienna, she had a first-hand knowledge of the avant-garde movements of Europe. When in Santiniketan, Kramrisch became an admirer of the nationalist painters of India, led by Abanindranath

Tagore and his pupil, Nandalal Bose. Later in life, Stella Kramrisch became a widely known authority on Indian art.

Rabindranath's worldwide reputation was also perhaps instrumental in inviting the Bauhaus artists of Germany to exhibit their work in Calcutta in December 1922. As the art historian Partha Mitter writes, it literally brought European Modernist art to the 'doorsteps of [our] city', which had till then known only Victorian academic art from the colonial masters.[8] What came out of it was also the influence of the Bauhaus association for reforming the art and craft education in the Santiniketan-Sriniketan trajectory. The Bauhaus school advocated the essential oneness of all things, and their appearances. They were not inclined to the pursuit of technology for progress as directed by the Industrial Revolution.

Rabindranath was deeply committed to the idea of inspiring freedom of expression and creativity in children's education. No wonder then that he went to meet one such leader of the Child Art Movement in Vienna, Franz Cizek (1865–1946, Austrian painter), during this same visit to Europe in 1921. What appealed to Rabindranath most of all in Cizek's ideas was with regard to the development of the 'whole' person in a child, and in developing his or her place in the wider environment.[9] Rabindranath also found a likeness in the ideas of the Bauhaus school founder, Walter Gropius (1883–1969, German architect), who wanted 'artists and craftsmen' to form a 'single art community'. The Bauhaus students followed an integrated course, which included painting, sculpture, architecture, design, and crafts. Both Gropius and Rabindranath believed that art and craft should play a vital role in social regeneration. In a fundamental way, that was Sriniketan's goal.

That goal was at its most distinctive through the evolution of artistic crafts in the history of Santiniketan and Sriniketan. Many of the crafts created at the two institutions were products of everyday use. They were often revived from lost traditions and made anew with aesthetically pleasing designs. The idea was to train the craftspersons to understand and accept that 'design' must have two components, art and purpose. The craftsmen did not have a problem with that idea or principle. They were clearly stimulated by the experience. The problem lay elsewhere and that was in the art society's rejection of craft as genuine art and delineating an inferior place to it in our society. That mindset was so deep-seated as to make even the 'established' artists nervous of losing their caste from working in the company of craftspersons or even running a joint training programme at par with them.

Both Rabindranath and Nandalal attempted to change this customary attitude to craft and craftspersons, at least in Santiniketan, but with only limited success. Workshops were started at Kala-Bhavana for training in some of the crafts. The outcome was that mural painting, sculpture, and other projects were undertaken, with a few of the teachers and the students working together, occasionally also getting a traditional artist or craftsperson to join them. Even with those arrangements in place, the atmosphere at Santiniketan was not conducive to an invigorating crafts movement. The training programme was therefore moved to Sriniketan, where it was made mandatory for every student in the institute's syllabus to learn at least one traditional craft, in addition to their chosen vocational training courses.

It is important to note that some of the handicrafts such as artistic leather craft, batik, and the fresco-buono technique were introduced for the first time in India at Santiniketan-Sriniketan by Rathi Babu and Pratima Devi (1893–1969, artist and Rathindranath's wife). It was during their Europe tour with Rabindranath in 1921, that Pratima Devi took courses in bookbinding and pottery. So far as batik was concerned, it was initiated by Surendranath Kar (1892–1970, architect of Santiniketan's early buildings), who had learned the process of making Indonesian-style batik, while he was travelling with Rabindranath in Java. In 1927,

Rabindranath went to Indonesia, Malaya, Java, Sumatra, and Siam. He was attracted to the batik craft, which he saw on their textiles and encouraged Surendranath Kar to pick up the art form during their tour.

On his return from Java, Surendranath taught the technique to Pratima Devi and Rathi Babu who were also very enthused by it. In fact, Rathi Babu experimented with it and tried out the technique on leather for the first time in artistic history. Santiniketan-Sriniketan became the celebrated home for leather batik. The Indonesian batik technique was, however, simplified at Santiniketan and the tools used were reduced. The Santiniketan designs were also different and distinctive from the Indonesian style. The Santiniketan form of batik came to be used as décor in Santiniketan's and Sriniketan's festivals. Nandalal Bose's daughters, Gauri (m. Bhanja, 1907–1998, artist) and Jamuna (m. Sen, 1912–2001, artist), created many beautiful designs on batik and popularized the form in creating Santiniketan's unique stage designs for honouring visitors or for performances. Indeed, the Santiniketan style of batik continues to this day to be sought after throughout India and much appreciated.

In the beginning, a tin shed was erected in Santiniketan where the crafts were going to be made. But shortly thereafter, all of that arrangement was moved to Sriniketan, when it became clear that the orthodox mentality of Santiniketan was not conducive for handicrafts to flourish there. It was clear that the Kala-Bhavana community of artists were not comfortable with accepting craft as an expression of pristine art. Initially, the crafts project was known by the name of 'Vichitra Studio'. After moving to Sriniketan, the training programme in crafts and the making of crafts were integrated in the Industries Department of Sriniketan and was housed in Silpa-Bhavana.[10]

There was some continuity in this development, given the fact that Birbhum had a past history of traditional craftsmanship in weaving and had enjoyed a good reputation in it. That was why Mr John Cheap, who was the East India Company's Commercial Resident of Birbhum from 1787 to 1828, could build a successful trade empire at Surul by exploiting the potential existing among the traditional weavers of Birbhum. (There is a chapter below on Sriniketan's Silpa-Bhavana with more information on this topic.)

As mentioned at the outset of the introduction, this book on Sriniketan's history has set out to document the work of rural reconstruction initiated at Sriniketan with its trials and errors, keeping in view the institution's foundational ideals. The chapters that follow will take us, first, into the biographical history of Rabindranath's close engagement with village reforms, starting with the work he began in his family estates. The chapter that will follow is about those beginnings. The title of the chapter is, 'Why Selidaha? Why Sriniketan? Why Rural Reconstruction?'

The rest of the chapters shall take us into the action from the field, alongside some discussions on the prevailing problems over land acquisition, peasant exploitation, village mentality, Sriniketan's aims and objectives, Sriniketan's agricultural and industrial development, Sriniketan's Department of Village Welfare, its educational projects starting with Siksha-Satra, the rural school, and Sriniketan's research work carried out through comprehensive village surveys, collection of economic data on village productivity, on the varieties and yields of rice, research on hygiene and sanitation, projects like introducing the Bored Hole Latrine, collection of statistics on malaria, research on measures for the prevention of malaria, and, not least of all, the making of the cooperative health societies across clusters of villages, starting from 1932.

The work carried out by the Sriniketan experiment was significant even if it was done on a limited scale. One could, of course, ask what would 10 or 15 advanced villages do for a country of the size of India? Rabindranath was not apologetic about the 'smallness of the work'.

What he earnestly wanted was to make 'at least a beginning' with the much-needed work of redeeming the Indian village from ruin. His hope was that someday, this work could become an ideal for the entire country. With the problems of 300 million people staring him in the face, he hoped that his efforts would touch at least the hearts of his rural neighbours and help them to reassert themselves in a bolder social order. Although he had joined the Swadesi Movement in 1904–05 wholeheartedly, and contributed a great number of patriotic songs that still move us, he left the movement as soon as it broke into sectarian riots, never ever to join it again. He became cynical of national enterprises and decided to work alone.

Rabindranath was not one to accept that all improvements had to wait for our country's political independence. He did not subscribe to that commonplace view. He believed that a great deal could be done by ourselves, for our own people, even with the colonial government at the helm. He acted upon the conviction that by making at least a beginning, we could shake off our characteristic inertia and take the lead to develop a progressive state of mind. 'Doing', he wrote, will also teach us to 'learn' what to 'do'. That is why he asked that the Sriniketan work be judged not by its size, but by its worth. He wrote:

> I alone cannot take responsibility for the whole of India. But even if two or three villages can be freed from the shackles of helplessness and ignorance, an ideal for the whole of India would be established.
>
> Fulfill this ideal in a few villages only, and I will say that these few villages are my India. And only if that is done, will India be truly ours.
>
> The scale of our enterprise will never be a matter of pride to us but let us hope its truth will be.[11]

Why Selidaha? Why Sriniketan? Why Rural Reconstruction?

> Among the politicians of those times, there was not one who regarded the rural people as members of our country. I said to a prominent leader of the Indian National Congress at the Pabna conference that the state can progress only if we pay attention to our lowly people, if we make an effort to transform their lives.[12]

In 1889–90, Rabindranath was sent by his father to take charge of the family's agricultural estates in East Bengal. The estates were owned by Rabindranath's grandfather, Dwarkanath Tagore (1794–1846, head of the Jorasanko Tagore family, pioneer entrepreneur, titled popularly as 'Prince' for his philanthropy), who was the first Indian to have founded a joint business venture with a British firm. In 1834, Dwarkanath launched the firm of Carr, Tagore & Co. He was congratulated by the then governor-general, Lord William Bentinck, for being the first Indian to start an Indo-British commercial enterprise. The firm supplied indigo and silk, and did business in coal mining, shipping, insurance, and banking. Dwarkanath's meteoric career took him from Bengal to Europe. He added spectacularly to the family estates and had many successes on his tour of Europe in 1842, when he dined with Queen Victoria at Buckingham Palace and had audiences with the Pope in Rome and with King Louis-Philippe in Paris. Dwarkanath's sudden death in England left the Jorasanko Branch of the Tagore family deeply in debt. The debt was paid off promptly by his son Debendranath Tagore (1817–1905, spiritual leader and co-founder of the reformist Hindu Movement known as the Brahmo Samaj), who was Rabindranath's father.

Even after repaying Dwarkanath Tagore's debts, the Tagore family retained some considerable proportion of their properties. There were six sprawling agricultural estates that spread out between Orissa and East Bengal. The estates in Orissa were in the Cuttack district. Those in East Bengal were at Sahajadpur in Pabna district, Kaligram in Rajsahi district, and Birahimpur in Nadia district. As the head of the Tagore family, Debendranath presided over these properties.

A time came when Debendranath asked his youngest son, Rabindranath, to leave Calcutta and move to the Birahimpur estates' headquarters at Selidaha on the banks of the mighty river, Padma, which was looked upon as the Ganga of East Bengal. The family houseboat called the Padma Boat was stationed at Selidaha and anchored at Selidaha's high banks. Writing from Selidaha in 1889, Rabindranath described the sandbanks that surrounded the houseboat as follows:

> Our house-boat is moored to a sandbank on the farther side of the river. A vast expanse of sand stretches away out of sight on every side, with here and there a streak, as of water, running across, though sometimes what gleams like water is only sand.
>
> Not a village, not a human being, not a tree, not a blade of grass—the only breaks in the monotonous whiteness are gaping cracks which in places show the layer of moist black clay underneath.
>
> Looking towards the East, there is endless blue above, endless white beneath. Sky empty, earth empty too—the

> emptiness below hard and barren, the overhead above arched and ethereal. One could hardly find anywhere such a picture of stark desolation.
>
> But on turning to the West, there is water, the currentless bend of the river, fringed with its high bank, up to which spreads the village groves with cottages peeping through—all like an enchanting dream in the evening light. I say 'evening light' because in the evening we wander out, and so that aspect is impressed on my mind. How extraordinary and beautiful our world really is: something easy to forget in Calcutta. When the sun sets each evening behind the peaceful trees along this small river, high above the boundless expanse of sand thousands and thousands of stars suddenly appear—you have to see it happen to grasp its wonder.[13]

Though stationed at the zamindari headquarters, Selidaha, Rabindranath travelled frequently to the other estates by the Padma Boat. He lived for days and nights on the boat. This was the first time in his life that he was seeing the countryside and coming into contact with the tenant farmers of the entire estate. They came to him as their landlord. He was eager to listen to their stories. He learned of their utter poverty and deep distress, and also of their many problems of cultivation and credit and marketing. He was deeply moved by their sad lives, but what he did not like was that they came to him as 'beggars'. They had no self-esteem.

We have a record of those experiences in his address to the workers of the Sriniketan Institute on his last visit there in 1939. He gave a personal and intimate account of what led him to start the work of rural reconstruction. That was why the address was published with the title 'Sriniketan er Itihas o Adorsho' (The History and Ideals of

Sriniketan). In that speech, he spoke of the shame he felt over his way of life as follows:

> The needs of my work took me on long distances from village to village, from Selidaha to Patisar, by rivers, large and small, and across 'beels' and in this way, I saw all the sides of village life. I was filled with eagerness to understand the villagers' daily routine and the varied pageant of their lives. I, the town-bred, had been received into the lap of rural loveliness and I began joyfully to satisfy my curiosity. Gradually, the sorrow and poverty of the villagers became clear to me, and I began to grow restless to do something about it. It seemed to me a very shameful thing that I should spend my days as a landlord, concerned only with money-making and engrossed with my own profit and loss. From that time forward, I continually endeavoured to find out how the villagers' minds could be aroused, so that they could themselves accept the responsibility for their own lives. If we merely offer them help from outside, it would be harmful to them. The critical question was to ask how they could be stirred to life. I was haunted by that thought and decided to act on it.[14]

Children living in hunger, and young women married as child brides and helplessly chained to their marriages felt to Rabindranath like a mockery of what human life should be. His tenants were mostly lower-caste Hindus and poor Muslims. Their everyday life was dismal and full of despair. Echoes of their pain perturbed Rabindranath deeply. He expressed those personal feelings vividly in a series of letters to his niece, Indira Devi Chaudhurani (1873–1960, author, daughter of Rabindranath's second brother, Satyendranath Tagore). The letters were later compiled into a volume and published in 1912 with the title *Chhinnopotro* (Torn Letters). In one of them, he wrote of a very deep 'inner' stirring, as follows:

> On that morning in the village the facts of my life suddenly appeared to me in a luminous unity of truth. All things that had seemed like vagrant waves were revealed to my mind in relation to a boundless sea. I felt sure that some Being who comprehended me and my world was seeking his best expression in all my experiences, uniting them into an ever-widening individuality which is a spiritual work of art. To this Being I was responsible; for the creation is His as well as mine…
>
> I felt that I had found my religion at last, the Religion of Man, in which the infinite became defined in humanity and came close to me so as to need my love and cooperation.[15]

It was this deeply felt compassion for the common man that turned him into a man of action physically, emotionally, and spiritually. That was how the Selidaha experience became so important to his self-development, his life work. The Selidaha estate was where Rabindranath's rural experiment began. A poem he wrote at the time, 'Ebar Phirao Morey' (Turn Me Back Now), speaks for itself. Here below is just one verse from the poem.

Come then, poet, rise,
If you have life, rally it, sacrifice it,
So much of pain and sorrow—afflicted world,
So poor, so empty, narrow, close and dark.
We want food, we want light, air to breathe free,

And health and strength, a long life lit with joy,
And breast made broad by courage. To this penury,
Poet, bring once from heaven an image of hope.[16]

To take the work forward, Rabindranath wrote his 'Swadeshi Samaj' (State and Society) essay of 1904–05. There, he gave a clarion call to the educated youth of Bengal to come and work in the villages. The idea proposed was that some of them would stay in the villages and work with the villagers towards building their *atmashakti* or self-reliance. A few young men responded indeed to the call and volunteered for the work. They lived in the villages in close contact with the people and started to organize them, so that they could jointly carry out such works as repairing roads and drains, excavating tanks, and clearing jungles. Prominent among them was Kalimohan Ghose (1884–1940, one of Rabindranath's closest associates in the Sriniketan work). Kalimohan responded to Rabindranath's call by coming at first to Selidaha from where he later moved to Santiniketan.

Among the landmarks from the early period of rural reconstruction in the family estates was the establishment of an agricultural bank at the Patisar estate in 1300 BC, c.1893–94. The bank was started to advance loans to the cultivators at approved rates and thus to relieve them from the exploitation of the money lender, the *mahajan*. Also, in some of the estates, new commercial crops were introduced, like the potato, and new businesses were started in jute and cloth and brick kilns. A sugar-crushing mill was started in Patisar. A weaving school was established near Selidaha in the town of Kushtia and special attention was given to the spread of education. Three schools were started in the estates and also a school for girls. Earlier, there were only two or three *tol*s for studying Sanskrit and a few *pathsala*s or primary schools. All these educational settings were run with funds from the Tagore estate.

After a decade's stay in East Bengal, Rabindranath moved to Santiniketanin in 1901 and continued with the village reform programme there. Santiniketan was where his father had founded a non-monastic ashram or a spiritual retreat in the 1860s. Debendranath was an ascetic by nature, a spiritual leader in his own right, and was popularly addressed as Maharshi. All the same, he carried out his householder's responsibilities fully, but took breaks from time to time and travelled to the Himalayas for spiritual succour. He travelled regularly from Calcutta to Amritsar and from there went up to the heights of the northern Himalayas, braving difficult terrain. But, as he became older, Debendranath sought a spiritual retreat closer to home, that is, closer to Calcutta. That is how he chose a spot, which became his 'Santiniketan' ashram, which he dedicated to the householders from all religions and backgrounds to spend time in prayer and meditation, away from their domestic responsibilities.

What we know today as the Santiniketan ashram was originally an empty spot deep in the interior of the district of Birbhum in the Rarh area of rural southern Bengal. It was inhabited by very old Hindu, Muslim, and Tribal villages that had links with the adjoining Santal Parganas. Shortly after establishing the Santiniketan ashram, Debendranath registered a trust deed to provide for its funding in the future. The trust included provisions for an annual village fair and for a school. This was the school that Rabindranath started in 1901 on moving with his family from Selidaha to Santiniketan. Two decades later, he added an international university to it for the study of the cultures of the East and the West. He named the university Visva-Bharati (World Learning). Its doors were thrown open to men and women from everywhere to collaborate in intellectual companionship and social action. Social action included a programme of rural reconstruction in the decaying villages surrounding the Santiniketan school. It was for that purpose that an institute of rural reconstruction was started at a village within two miles of the Santiniketan school and named 'Sriniketan', an abode of beauty.

The steady decay of the villages from the late 19th century was mainly due to the migration of the newly English-educated Indian elite from the villages to the city. This elite were men who were qualified in the professions and preferred to leave their ancestral villages for jobs or independent practice in the city. This was a big change for the villages, because the tradition over the ages had been that the landed gentry did all the welfare work for their poor tenant farmers. They were the traditional 'guardians' to whom the charge of their village was handed down from generation to generation. They arranged for all the necessities, whether it was to do with excavating the tanks or building the temples. Society had mandated that the wealthy and the upper castes would have to spend their wealth for the needs of the society. It was only after fulfilling those obligations to the needy that the 'guardians' could spend their wealth as they wished. This was how the overall responsibility for the well-being of the villagers belonged to the elite.

While this societal arrangement had provided the village people with their basic physical needs, it had at the same time stripped them of their self-reliance, and indeed, any sense of *atmashakti*. They remained complacent over their miserable state of life. They ascribed their miseries to their inborn karma. They blissfully convinced themselves that there was no escape from their suffering. Rabindranath recalled some of this mentality among the villagers when he wrote:

> In my estate the river was far away and lack of water was a serious problem. I said to my tenants, 'If you dig a well, I shall get it cemented'. Their reaction was plain and simple. 'You want to fry fish in the oil of the fish itself. If you dig the

> well you will go to heaven through the accumulated virtue of having provided the thirsty with water whereas we shall have done the work.' Their idea, obviously, was that an account of all such deeds was kept in heaven and while I, having earned great merit, could go to the seventh heaven, the village people would just get some water.[17]

The consequences inevitably were a further widening of the social and economic gap between town and country, city and village. The villagers lived in a perpetual muddle. They were without a clue about what was expected of them. They had no notion about what it was to live with responsibility and self-respect. It was no surprise, therefore, that the villages went into decline in the course of time. Cholera and malaria became virulent in village after village and the springs of happiness dried up. Rabindranath felt determined to intervene in that decline, in spite of his limited resources.

He knew well that a civilization that comprises of only village life could not be sustained in the modern age. 'Rustic was a synonym for the mind's narrowness', he wrote.[18] He sought, therefore, to bring the village and the city close by means of an endeavour to combine traditional knowledge with scientific experiment. In modern times, the city had become the repository of the 'new' knowledge. Rabindranath had the prescience to believe that it was essential for the village to cooperate with the city, in order to access the new knowledge. His study of 'other agricultural countries' had shown how land in those countries had been made to yield twice or thrice by the use of science. In Sriniketan, as in his agricultural estates earlier, he attempted to introduce the latest techniques to improve cultivation, including the use of farm machinery. A motor tractor was bought for Sriniketan in 1927, as recorded in the institute's Minute Book for 1922–32. He wrote with great expectation,

'If we can possess the science that gives power to this age, we may yet win, we may yet live.'[19]

The other important goal for Sriniketan was to organize the villages so that they could supply all their needs on a cooperative basis. The idea was that, given education, the villagers would be able to establish and maintain their own schools and granaries, their banks and cooperative stores. It was thought that the ties of cooperation would unite the village people and free them from dependence on the 'city' and the 'government'. That would also be the self-respecting way of resolving the issue of alienation between the common people and the upper classes. Rabindranath's intervention was to bring about this much-needed change for his society's self-respect. By change in this regard, he meant, first and foremost, a change of attitude. He thus wrote, 'It is not enough to try to remove wants; you can never remove them completely from outside; the far greater thing is to rouse the will of the people to remove their own wants.'[20]

Rabindranath abhorred the contempt of the Bengali intelligentsia for the masses. They regarded the common people as *chhotolok*, literally, people of low class. With extreme sarcasm he asked, how could the common people be anything other than lowly, given that their own high society never felt any compassion for them? With deep disappointment Rabindranath wrote, 'There have been many a movement among our common people, but that remains unknown to our students. They do not want to know because it does not fetch them pass marks in examinations.'[21] He ridiculed the Bengali college student who studied economics and ethnology with their European teachers in order to learn of the customs and laws of their very own village next door.

The Sriniketan Work Begins

> Please take it seriously when I say that my whole heart is with you in the great work you have started. I wish I were young enough to be able to join you and perform the meanest work that can be done in your place, thus getting rid of the filmy web of respectability that shuts me off from intimate contact with Mother Dust. It is something unclean like prudery itself to have a sweeper to serve that deity who is in charge of the primal cradle of life.[22]

Rabindranath sent the above note to the Sriniketan pioneer L.K. Elmhirst on 31 March 1922, when he learned that the first batch of Surul students had dug trenches in their own backgardens to dump the night soil to help in the improvement of agriculture. Rabindranath very eagerly looked forward to the day when his village work would benefit from the contributions of modern science. In as early as 1906, he sponsored three young men from Santiniketan to study agriculture and dairy farming at the University of Illinois, Urbana-Champaign, in the USA. They were his son Rathi, his son-in-law Nagendranath Ganguli (1889–1958, married to Rabindranath's youngest daughter Mira Devi), and his friend Srishchandra Majumdar's son, Santosh Chandra Majumdar (1886–1926, student of the Santiniketan school, and afterwards, teacher too). The plan was that at the end of their higher studies in agricultural sciences, they would bring their newly acquired knowledge to the work of rural reconstruction in India.

Rabindranath felt sure from his observation of other agricultural countries that the economic salvation of the village lay in the application of expertise. In 1909, all the three graduates from the University of Illinois returned with their state-of-the-art training in agriculture and animal husbandry and began to introduce scientific methods to the Sriniketan work. Their experiments were carried out jointly with the villagers.

To take the work forward, Rabindranath bought 20 bighas of land in 1912, along with a house that stood on that plot of land just outside the village called Surul, within two miles west of Santiniketan, where the Sriniketan Institute was to be located. The house that stood on the land was commonly known as 'Cheap Kuthi'. It belonged to the East India Company's Commercial Resident for the District of Birbhum, John Cheap, who lived in it from 1787 to 1828. His job was to indent the local supply of cotton and silk fabrics on the Company's account with an annual investment quota of 45,000 to 65,000 in Pounds Sterling. Silk and cotton fabrics comprised the major portion of the East India Company's advances. The weavers used to work on a system of 'advances', all of which was handled by the Company's Commercial Resident.[23]

As Commercial Resident, the punctual supply of the Company's requirements was the main job. For that, good cooperation was needed from the local agents. Mr Cheap found Surul and its neighbourhood not only rich in raw materials, but he also found a friend and ally in an influential landlord cum businessman of Surul, Sri Srinivas Sarkar. It was from the Sarkars that John Cheap obtained a vast tract of land, on which he built his palatial house surrounded by a garden and an orchard. It was an impressively large house, but fallen into ruin by the time Rabindranath bought the property. The fact that John Cheap was posted at the place by the East India Company was proof of the earlier prosperity of the region.[24]

John Cheap encouraged spinning and weaving in the villages around. He collected his produce, as well as the other goods for sale, through a network of huge clearing stations. It is believed that his enterprise brought the whole area to a level of prosperity, which was seen in a sprouting of 'pukka' buildings, houses, and temples. Machine-spun cloth with identical patterns, copied from Cheap's exported goods, began to reach the Port of Calcutta at cut rates. But the inevitable outcome was that Birbhum's hand-woven cloths were thrown out of the market. As a result, the villages were ultimately reduced to poverty and infested with the diseases of cholera and malaria. This was also the time when the district was getting its first railway line. The massive digging undertaken by the East India Railways in laying the Bolpur Line had an adverse impact on the environment and the people's health.

For the first few years of the Sriniketan work, nothing substantial could be done with that plot of land except to clear the jungles surrounding the area of 'Cheap Kuthi' and to meet the villagers. A scheme was also started to make the Surul farm into a model for the benefit of the cultivators living in the surrounding villages. This holistic task was led by Rathi Babu and Nagendranath Ganguli, who, armed as it were, with their study and training at the University of Illinois were ready to make an impact on rural reconstruction. But nothing came of those early attempts to start the work in earnest, because all the workers came down with malaria. That is how the initial 10 years were spent like a roller coaster with starting the work and stopping it at intervals.

In 1921, Rabindranath travelled widely to inform the larger humanity about his Visva-Bharati International University at Santiniketan, a 'place' for the world to meet as in a single 'nest'. When he was in the USA, he arranged to meet a young Englishman who was then a student of agriculture at Cornell University. This was L.K. Elmhirst (1893–1974, agricultural economist, led the Sriniketan work during 1922–24, and later gave it his lifelong support). Rabindranath had been told about Elmhirst by another Englishman, Sam Higginbottom (1874–1958), who founded the Nainital Agricultural Institute, where Elmhirst had worked for some months as a wartime volunteer in 1917–18. Rabindranath appealed to Elmhirst to come over and start the Surul Farm.

About their meeting Elmhirst wrote:

> I remember well the morning in the spring of 1921 when a telegram reached me at Ithaca, from Tagore, which read 'Come and see me in New York. I made a hurried journey to New York, and shall never forget the friendly welcome I received. 'I have', Tagore said to me, 'an institution of learning and the arts at Santiniketan which is mainly academic. It is surrounded by villages, some Hindu, some Muslim, some Santal, but all are decaying; all had an ancient culture, but today they appear sick. Will you come and help me to find out why? Would you be prepared to go and live in a village? Would you like to consider it? Then how about sailing back with me tomorrow?'
>
> 'But', said I, 'if I am really to be of any use to you, I must finish my course at Cornell'.[25]

Elmhirst came to work for Sriniketan after completing his course of studies at Cornell. He came to Santiniketan at the end of 1921 and started the rural work in 1922, by moving to Surul with a team of two teachers and 10 senior students from the Santiniketan school. In the team were Rathi Babu, Santosh Majumdar, and Kalimohan Ghose, whom Elmhirst referred to as his 'three closest collaborators'. Another resource person who joined them soon after was Miss Gretchen Green from the USA, a paramedical nurse, who was asked to set up the Village Health Centre and Clinic at Surul.[26]

It was not easy at first for the Santiniketan-Sriniketan team to start their work as there was an ongoing political movement at the time. Gandhi's Non-cooperation Movement had touched many hearts, even in Santiniketan. The political ferment also affected the team's relationship with the villagers to some extent. Elmhirst wrote in his diary how Rabindranath used to discuss their local problems and experiences regularly and consulted, in particular, with Kalimohan Ghose, as he was the Sriniketan contact person with the local villagers. Moreover, the villagers trusted Kalimohan Ghose.

Initially, the team took up reconstruction work in the three designated villages in Surul's neighbourhood. The records in Elmhirst's diary refer to the desperate struggle they had in making the initial contacts, at first, with the Muslim villages, and later, also with the Hindu villages. Again, as Elmhirst wrote in his diaries, Rabindranath learned about it all from Kalimohan and gave his encouragement to keep the work going and reiterated his support for it.[27]

After getting the work started, Elmhirst could stay for only two years, from 1922 to 1924. He had to return to England to start his own educational institution, Dartington Hall in Devonshire, though he remained connected with the Sriniketan work throughout his life. His correspondence with Rathi Babu bears out how closely he followed all matters of Sriniketan, even criticized some of it in his assessment. Rathi Babu sought Elmhirst's advice earnestly, and a number of the leading village workers also stayed in touch with him. Elmhirst himself returned to Sriniketan on short visits every couple of years. The lady he married, Dorothy Whitney Straight (1887–1958), endowed an annual grant of Rs 32,000 for Sriniketan, which was of foundational help to the work over the years. That is how Sriniketan's 'permanence' was ensured. Dorothy Whitney Straight was the daughter of the American financier, William Whitney, and the widow of the distinguished diplomat Willard Straight. Rabindranath dedicated his book of essays, *Pioneer in Education,* to Dorothy with the following words, 'To Dorothy Whitney Straight who made Sriniketan possible'[28].

When the Sriniketan work was being conceived, Rabindranath insisted on an all-rounded approach that would take account of the villager's life in all aspects. He also asserted his confidence in the cooperation of the young people in bringing about the reforms and in gradually taking along their elders with them to that end. That is why he was attracted to the Scout Movement founded by Lieutenant General Robert Baden-Powell (1857–1941, founder of the worldwide Scout Movement), and decided to tie up the Sriniketan experiment with the Scout Movement.[29] Rathi Babu arranged for two boys from the Santiniketan school to join a training course for Scout leaders in the Central Provinces.

Among the other aspects of the Sriniketan experiment, Rabindranath encouraged the collaboration of scientists, economists, sociologists, and technicians with the work. He encouraged one and all to stand by the villagers in their struggle against poverty and oppression. He was also cautious that the team did not impose too much 'statistics' or technicalities on the villagers in bringing about the changes. He wrote to Elmhirst, 'All the time when Sriniketan has been struggling to grow into a form, I was intently wishing that it should not only have a shape, but also light, so that it might transcend its immediate limits of time, space and special purpose.'[30]

Rabindranath also asked for the cooperative principle to be introduced into the Sriniketan reforms. The idea was to educate the villagers to value the cooperative effort to start their own schools, workshops, granaries, their own cooperative stores, and to learn to maintain them. He explained that we must try to combine all our labour power, in order to gain social and economic benefits that could be shared by all. He believed that isolation had kept the villages weak and backward. He wrote, 'Our salvation lies in making our villages knit together by the ties of cooperative life.'[31]

On the other hand, Rabindranath knew instinctively that a cooperative way of life would succeed only by means of a new and alternative education. He hoped that such an education could create a new Indian personality capable of reaching out into India's past, but capable also of finding itself in the universe where minds meet. This Indian personality would be equal with the best in the history of humanity as one belonging to a great nation, free of the conflict of communities and integrated with the universe of men, not weak and begging as was the nature of the 19th century Indian gentlemen educated in a Western style.

Santiniketan had students from both urban and rural families. Rabindranath's ideas for a 'new' education were founded on exposing the urban student to the culture and traditions of the village and the rural student to the city as the repository of modern knowledge. While the village housed the majority of India's populace, the city became the new home for the English educated. It was essential, therefore, for the city and the village to cooperate for the development of the new Indian personality. Rabindranath insisted on the necessity for this change.

He did not, however, fail to see that the country's education was going in the 'opposite' direction from his ideas. Far from any of the changes envisaged by Rabindranath, 'national' education was becoming more like a machine to create jobs for the colonial administration as the principal aim. The newly educated Indian middle class were seriously lured by the prospect of jobs in the colonial government. Education seemed of no other worth to them. Rabindranath observed how different that was from what was being done in Russia to educate the masses. He saw for himself how hundreds and thousands became educated within a decade of the Russian Revolution. He, of course, knew why. He knew that the contrast was due to the mentality of his own middle class society, who did not seriously care for their own people. Their social commitment was limited to their utterances at the meetings of the Indian National Congress or in the articles they wrote for the newspapers. Rabindranath pointed out that those so-called 'words of wisdom' did nothing for the country to grow.

All through his life, he championed the need to impart education for the masses. In his essays, 'Lokahita' (People's Welfare) and 'Sikshar Bikiron' (The Spread of Education), Rabindranath explained that the welfare of the people could be safeguarded only if they were made literate.[32] He lamented that our rural folk were not conscious of their own strength. That was why they could not make their strength felt to others. He pointedly added that the upper classes of our society could live in such comfort and complacency, only because the common people had surrendered their human rights and chose to remain subservient. That was why they could be blatantly exploited by the zamindar, the money lender, the revenue officer, and the police.

Rabindranath was determined to bring change by means of an ideal education at Santiniketan and Sriniketan. He believed such an education could help in the making of a new Indian personality bearing a social conscience. To his disappointment, he saw that did not happen. He criticized the Santiniketan education for having become 'borrowed cages that treated the students' minds as captive birds'. He turned his hopes to Sriniketan. In a letter to Elmhirst on

19 December 1937, he reiterated his ideas of what he expected from an ideal centre of education at Sriniketan:

> Dear Leonard,
>
> You know how for a long time I have been cherishing my hope of establishing an ideal centre of education at Sriniketan—an ideal which is not curtailed to the strictest measure of a narrow village environment, which is not specially set apart to be doled out as famine ration carefully calculated to be just good enough for emaciated life and dwarfed mentality. It is well known that the education which is prevalent in our country is extremely meagre in the spread of its area and barren in quality. Unfortunately, this is all that is available for us and that has set up an artificial standard proudly considered as respectable. Outside the '*bhadralok*' class, pathetic in their struggle for fixing a university label on their name, there is a vast obscure multitude who cannot even dream of such a costly ambition. With them we have our best opportunity if we know how to use it, and there only we can have our freedom for offering to our country the best all-round culture not mutilated by the official dictators. I have generally noticed that when the charitably minded city-bred politicians talk of education for the village folk they mean a little left-over in the bottom of their cup after diluting it copiously. They are callously unmindful of the fact that the kind and the amount of food that is needful for the mental nourishment must not be apportioned differently according to the social status of those that receive it.

Sriniketan should be able to provide for its pupils an atmosphere of rational thinking and behaviour which alone can save them from stupid bigotry and moral cowardliness. I myself attach much more significance to the educational possibilities of Siksha-Satra, than to the school and college of Santiniketan, which are everyday becoming more and more like so many schools and colleges elsewhere in this country, borrowed cages that treat the student's minds as captive birds whose sole human value is judged according to the mechanical repetition of lessons prescribed by an education dispensation foreign to the soil.

With my affectionate regards,
Ever yours,
Rabindranath Tagore[33]

The Land Problem, Nationalists, and Rabindranath

> May we never have to burden the poor peasants on the land for maintaining us in food and comfort. I have been saying this for such a long time. It has been my hope that our zamindari should belong to the peasants themselves, we should be their trustees. Some allowance for livelihood we can claim from them, but only as partners…that I could not achieve this makes me sad. But it will be shameful if we give up the attempt.[34]

If we take the goal of self-reliance or *atmashakti* as a basic premise in Rabindranath's ideal for rural reconstruction, it would help us to understand the difference between his Sriniketan experiment and the nationalist and economic thinking of his day. The difference was over the remedies, though the Indian National Congress was also concerned about the decline of rural India. For example, whereas the Indian National Congress decided to pass on the work of village reform to the colonial government, Rabindranath insisted that it was the absolute duty of the educated Indians to provide the nation-building services to the people. He believed that could also be a means of correcting the alienation that was growing between the urban middle class and the rural populace. But the Congress merely engaged themselves in writing petitions to the government to seek favours for the country.

Rabindranath criticized the Congress for its 'politics of begging'. In a letter of 1312 (c.1906) to the intellectual stalwart, Ramendra Sundar Trivedi (1864–1919, author and intellectual), Rabindranath shared his criticism of the Congress policy as follows:

> You may take it for certain that those who lose sight of the higher ideals and regard a boastfully self-assertive attitude towards the government as the best means of cultivating our own strength and mistake it for the foundation of our own power, those who look upon the establishment of a national education foundation as nothing but a manifestation of that attitude, [they] will never be able to render any abiding service to the country. If at the present moment such people are actually in a majority in the country and their influence is in the ascendant, then it should be the duty of people like ourselves to devote our attention quietly to our own work. I have therefore resolved not to get excited over the preparation for a conflagration and shall wait, as long as I live, patiently on the road-side with my own light burning.[35]

Rabindranath's independent thinking gave him the courage of conviction to disagree with the Congress and work with his own ideas of 'constructive swadeshi' with village reform at the grassroots. He had felt the urge to work for the village people from seeing their sorrows at close quarters during living and working among his tenant farmers. He continued with the same urge after moving to Santiniketan and seeing the same miserable conditions in the villages surrounding the Santiniketan school. In a letter in 1910 to his son Rathindranath, he expressed his disillusionment over the 'national' programme. He wrote, 'A deep despair now pervades rural life all over the country, so much so that high-sounding phrases like home rule, autonomy, etc. appear to me almost ridiculous and I feel ashamed even to utter them. I was one of the principal organisers of the National Fund and now I feel conscious stricken about it.'[36]

He had come to the conclusion that working for a 'national' programme was useless as long as the urban middle class was divided and there was a conflict of vested interests among them. At the same time, he also felt that there was a widespread sensitivity to nation-building among the general public. His experience of the National Fund was an eye-opener in this regard, because there he saw directly how a hefty sum was collected in one single day despite the low incomes of the donors themselves. It was clear, he wrote, that the people were keen to 'give' for the nation. Moved by this direct experience, he included the message in his address to the Pabna Provincial Conference of Bengal in 1908 by declaring:

> The people of the land are anxious to give and to work. They therefore want to know to whom to give, and what. If we cannot direct the urges of the country along the right channels, if everything is done in a haphazard and unorganised manner, is it surprising that men should feel frustrated and dissipate their energy in fratricidal quarrels?[37]

There was also concern over the issue of landlordism. There too there was a difference between Rabindranath and the Indian National Congress. In the early phase of the Congress, the majority opinion was in favour of landlordism and the demand was for the extension of the 1793 Permanent Settlement of Bengal. An attempt was made towards a total change of land-relations later in the 20s and 30s. This happened when a demand was made for zamindari abolition and the 'appropriation of land without compensation' from the Workers and Peasants Party, the Congress Socialists, and the Kisan Sabha elements.[38]

Such a situation arose because the Permanent Settlement of 1793 created a class of hereditary zamindars in Bengal. They were given the right to a share in the produce of the land, irrespective of whether or not they took part in the productive process. When the government realized the consequences, there was no scope for going back. The tenants soon found it more profitable to rent out their holdings to sub-tenants, who were sometimes complete newcomers, without any knowledge about agriculture and its requirements. Moreover, the collection of rents from every layer was so structured that a substantial portion of the produce was reserved for the tenants who did not perform any agricultural labour.

In the final analysis, the actual cultivator was left with an unpaid initial debt to the moneylender, which kept accumulating. To deal with this accumulation, the direct cultivator was forced to sell a very high portion of his produce 'in distress' by sacrificing his own need. Ruined as he already was, the cultivator was set back further by having to borrow all over again in order to buy paddy for his own subsistence and to make that last till the next harvest. For most peasants, this vicious circle plunged them into mounting indebtedness. Either that, or they had to take the ultimate recourse of the transfer of peasant holdings on a considerable scale.

These apprehensions were clearly stated by Rabindranath in a foreword he wrote for the essay titled *Ryot er Kotha* (About the Peasant) authored by Pramatha Chaudhuri (1868–1946, litterateur, married to Rabindranath's niece, Indira Devi Chaudhurani).[39] The essay had made out a case in favour of 'peasant proprietorship'. In his foreword, Rabindranath explained why peasant proprietorship would not succeed while land was being used as a commodity for buying and selling in an open market economy. He forewarned that even the peasants themselves would plunge into the 'grab' for land if they got an opportunity to do so. Such a possibility was bound to result in further depletion and fragmentation of the land that was left for cultivation. Rabindranath also warned of the very likelihood that the inheritors of landed property could take advantage of the situation and rush in to claim their inheritances. In such a multiple race for land, the amount left with the actual cultivator would not suffice even for his domestic needs. His poverty would force him into further transfers of land and distress sales.

Rabindranath further warned that even the minimal rights of the peasant under the zamindar's regime would be destroyed by the combined power of the zamindar and the moneylender. In his own zamindari, therefore, he took a radically different route as landlord. He worked directly with the peasants, irrespective of what the nationalists thought or the government did.

Rabindranath knew well how desperate the land problem was. His concern was primarily over human 'attitudes'. For example, it did not perturb him particularly that the landlord took rent even from the poor tenants, because he knew that extracting rent was 'second nature' to landlordism. But it distressed him seriously if the landlord shirked the 'moral' responsibility for the welfare of his tenants. It distressed him seriously if the landlord did not protect his tenants from the extortionists, such as the moneylenders, the policemen, and the revenue collectors. He knew that given how their manhood had been suppressed over the ages, the lowly tenant farmers could not possibly stand on their feet if they had to forever live at the mercy of the extortionists.

A zamindar himself by family heritage, Rabindranath was more than aware of his country's social injustices. He knew only too well of the general oppression inflicted on the tenants by the zamindars, as was characteristic of any feudal society. That was why he blamed the Congress for diverting attention from the greater need for social justice compared to the excitement over nationalist politics. Rabindranath's work as a zamindar in the Tagore family estate was put on record in the District Gazetteers of the period as follows:

> It must not be imagined that a powerful landlord is always oppressive and uncharitable. A striking instance is given in the Settlement Officer's account of the estate of Rabindranath Tagore. The Settlement Officer pointed out how honesty and fair dealing on the part of the estate employees had been strictly enforced, how rent remission had been generously granted to deserving cases, and how education was encouraged and a charitable dispensary run.[40]

The Mentality of the Villages

> If we merely offer them help from outside, it would be harmful to them. How could they themselves be stirred to life? That question gave me much food for thought. It was difficult to help them because they despised themselves. They would say, 'We are dogs—only whipping and beating will keep us right'.[41]

Those heartbreaking words in English translation are from Rabindranath's 1939 address to the Sriniketan Institute of Rural Reconstruction, titled 'Sriniketan er Itihas o Adorsho', which was translated into English as 'The History and Ideals of Sriniketan'. He saw for himself the deplorable condition of the Bengal countryside, particularly the state of the district of Birbhum, where the Sriniketan work of rural reconstruction was based. There was an acute problem over the condition of the soil in Birbhum. In 1923, Elmhirst gave a public lecture in Calcutta on the subject, titled 'The Robbery of the Soil and Rural Reconstruction', over which Rabindranath presided. In the lecture, Elmhirst pointed out that the village soil was badly destroyed, because it was continuously 'drained' of its properties, but never replenished. The problem had got worse at the turn of the century because of Birbhum's proximity to the large city of Calcutta with its growing population and growing demand for food. To top it all, Birbhum was also suffering from 'malaria, monkeys, and mistrust', the 'three M-s', as Elmhirst referred to it.

Yet, there was a time when Surul had the reputation of being a healthy place and free of the scourge of malaria. That was no longer the case when the Sriniketan experiment was being set up. A spleen index carried out by the Sriniketan Institute showed that 80 out of 95 villagers were living with enlarged spleens. As a consequence, they had lost the capacity for manual work to a considerable extent.

The villagers' mentality was another deeply discouraging factor. Their lives were steeped in apathy and suspicion of the unfamiliar. To illustrate how desperate the situation was, Rabindranath described an incident from his first-hand experience in the early days of the Sriniketan work. One day, a fire broke out in a neighbouring village. At first, the concerned villagers did nothing about it. Others came from a neighbouring Muslim village and put the fire out. It was only then that some of the local villagers came and joined the effort to put out the fire. As there was no water available, they were asked to break down the roofs of the houses to bring the fire under control. Their apathy was so great that the Sriniketan staff had to give them a few physical blows to make them pull down the houses. Rabindranath wrote, 'After the fire was over they came to me and said how fortunate it was that the "*babus*" had broken down their houses so that the people of the village could be saved. They were very pleased and admitted readily that the blows of the "*babus*" were for their good; but I myself felt ashamed.'[42]

Rabindranath added another story of their mentality from his Selidaha days. He had built a road all the way from Selidaha to Kushtia, where the Tagore estate office was situated, and asked the villagers to take charge of the responsibility for the upkeep of the road. The bullock carts they plied on that road created ruts and potholes, making the road unsuitable in the rains. He asked them to work together to put the road back into shape. To that the reaction of the villagers was, 'We are asked to repair the road so that the "*babus*" can go and come in comfort.' Rabindranath realized that their mentality was such that they could not bear the thought of anyone getting any benefit from their actions other than themselves. They rather preferred to put up with the inconvenience of a broken road themselves! He thus wrote, 'It is very difficult to help such people.'[43]

There were other difficulties with regard to bringing change to the village mentality. Historically speaking, India's villages had always been isolated as part of their way of life. They either liked it the way it was or had got completely accustomed to it as the only way of life. This ancient habit had left them with a suspicious mentality about the 'outsider' and all things from 'outside' the familiar confines of their life. Over and above, there was also their dependence on and adherence to the outdated caste rules.

The worst of it was how the zamindari system took advantage of all of those problems at the cost of the villager's wellbeing. They did so deliberately. The upper-caste people owned a lot of land, but did not do any work with their hands. The result was that there was a preponderance of tenants and sharecroppers which hampered efficient farming. It had led to the fragmentation of the landholdings. Those difficulties were compounded by the Hindu Law of Inheritance which supported the zamindari system. Therefore, Rabindranath knew that any remedy over land ownership was beyond the reach of any 'rural reconstruction' projects. But he also firmly believed that an effort had to be made to circumvent the problems, so as to bring some relief to the peasantry. He knew there was no way of upsetting the existing land rights. He did not also intervene in the villager's traditional constraints.

Given all those impediments, it is understandable why the Sriniketan scheme of rural reconstruction was not directed towards revolutionary change in the economic and social structure of the country. However pioneering the work, the idea was to let it evolve from within society. The thrust was for a change of attitude. Rabindranath consistently argued that only those changes would endure that had been brought about from a change in human psychology. In other words, it would have to be a change from within the individual, and from within the society itself. He wrote, 'Any teaching concerning man must have human nature for its chief element. How far it will harmonise with human nature is a matter of time.'[44]

Srinketan's ideals followed from those principles. One such practical effect was seen to succeed in tackling the monkey problem in the villages. Here, we have the evidence of how a 'change of attitude' led to a distinct change in the economic life of the village. One of the reasons of rural poverty was that a second crop could not be grown after harvesting the rice crop in November–December, because the moneys invariably destroyed the crop. Even then, the villagers did not kill the monkeys due to some customary superstition. Initially, the Sriniketan team were diffident about asking the villagers to give up such an old superstition. But they pursued the matter all the same and succeeded. They initiated a dialogue with a number of the villagers, which of course took time and plenty of negotiation. The villagers finally agreed to 'kill' monkeys for the larger cause of increasing the production of food grain.

As an overall strategy to break out of some of those prevalent disadvantages, Elmhirst designed and launched an experiment to involve the younger generation of villagers, which he named 'Education and Experience'. He learned from direct experience that the village elders took an interest if they saw their youngsters taking part in something new. One example was in the effort to clean up the villages by arming the young village boys with effective tools for the job and taking them along with the Sriniketan team to do it. To everyone's delight, the elders voluntarily joined in. Elmhirst wrote:

> So long as we had the confidence, cooperation, and trust of the parent, and so long as they felt that the children would come to no harm in our hands, we decided to concentrate on the boys and girls. Among the tragedies of the world is the blindness of average parents to the welfare of their children. Our chief discovery, and our hope perhaps, is the rapidity with which the parent learns from the child when the child has something good to show.[45]

It was clear that Rabindranath's major objective in rural reconstruction was to inspire a degree of synergy into the overall life of the village. He expected, of course, that improved cultivation and increased production would be the first step in the process. But he knew instinctively that there had to be something more to cheer up life in the villages. He wrote:

> Speaking of the villages I know personally, I may say they are absolutely appalling in their total joylessness. Gone without trace are 'jatra', 'kathaka', 'kirtan', and other aids to folk education, and folk entertainment. Those who patronized these have either left the village or their sense of values have undergone a complete reorientation. The village folk are no longer able to benefit from what knowledge we had acquired or amassed; or rather, we are no more able to plough back our stored knowledge into the soil of their mind. Their mental life is no longer enlivened with music and ballads and tales.[46]

In a letter that he wrote in 1915 to Atul Sen, an estate worker in his Kaligram estate, he explained what he wanted for the village, which was as follows:

> I have something else to urge upon you. A note of joy has to be sounded in all your work. Village life has become very dull. The dryness of the heart has to be banished. All welfare work ought to be turned as far as possible into an occasion of festive joy. There should be a tree-planting ceremony every year. I think you will have to give your students a day off sometime at the end of the month of 'Vaisakh' and organize a picnic in a forest coupled with a tree-planting ceremony. If a festive element is introduced on the day in which a new work is started, such as the construction of a road is launched, a religious appearance will be imparted to all your social activities.
>
> Another thing should be borne in mind. It will do a lot of good to the villager if he can be induced to take to the hobby of cultivating flowers. A few '*bel*' or a few rose plants, if grown in the yard of every cottage, will make the villages look beautiful. Let us not forget that this cultivation of beauty has become a very great necessity in our country.[47]

The aim surely was 'life in its completeness' and, again, not by charity, but by cooperation. He wanted the deprived to become self-sufficient and self-reliant, by taking charge of their needs by themselves on a cooperative basis. Rabindranath wrote, 'We must so endeavour that a power from within the villagers themselves may be working alongside us, even if that was not discernible by us. This idea formulated itself in my mind when I wrote "Swadeshi Samaj". If we merely offer to help them from outside it would be harmful to them.'[48]

He was full of tenderness for his tenants, and full of affection for the hapless peasant. He understood with depth and humility their problems from birth and how their manhood had suffered. In a letter he wrote to his niece, Indira Devi Chaudhurani, from Selidaha on 11 May 1893, he expressed his feelings for the tenants poignantly, thus:

> When our old ryots come to see me here their reverence is so unaffected. The simplicity and sincerity of their devotion makes them much greater than me. Though unworthy of the devotion as I am, that does not devalue it.
>
> I feel the same kind of love for these grown up children as I do for little children—with a particular difference. These big children are the more childlike; for the little children will grow up in due course, but the big children never will. Meek and gentle souls shine within their ravaged and wrinkled bodies. The souls of little children are merely simple, without this calm unquestioning faith. If currents of intuition really do link human beings, then I hope the good wishes in my heart will reach these ryots' hearts and help them.
>
> Of course not all tenants are like this: that would be too much to expect. Whatever is finest is always rare.[49]

Aims, Objects, and Activities of Sriniketan

> Our task at Sriniketan was to try and give effect and form to what so many thought were only a poet's idle dreams. Few people realised how fundamental and practical Tagore's ideas were about the village and its needs.[50]

From its outset, the Sriniketan Institute of Rural Reconstruction was organized under a democratic Executive Committee or 'Karma Samiti' as it was named by Visva-Bharati. This committee represented several local workers and eminent personalities from India and abroad. The institute drew up its aims and objects[51] as follows:

- To win the friendship and affection of the villagers and the cultivators by taking a real interest in all that concerns their life and welfare, and by making a lively effort to assist them in solving their most pressing problems.
- To take the problems of the village and the field to the classroom for study and discussion and to the experimental farm for solution.
- To carry the knowledge and experience gained in the classroom and the experimental farm to the villagers in the endeavour to improve their sanitation and health, to develop their resources and credit, to help them sell their produce and buy their requirements to their best advantage, to teach them better methods of growing crops and

vegetables and of keeping livestock, to encourage them to learn and practice arts and crafts, and to bring home to them the benefits of a united life, mutual aid, and common endeavour.

- To work out practically an all-round system of elementary education in the villages, based on the Boy Scout principles and training, with the object of developing ideas of citizenship and public duty, such as may appeal to the villagers and be within their means and capacity.
- To encourage among the staff and students of the department itself a spirit of sincere service and willing sacrifice in the interests of and on terms of comradeship with their poorer, less educated, and greatly harassed neighbours in the villages.
- To lead the students towards a due sense of their own intrinsic worth, physical and moral, and in particular, to teach them from the start to do everything which a village householder or a cultivator does for a living, if possible, more efficiently.
- To arrange for the students to acquire practical experience in cultivation, dairy keeping, animal husbandry, poultry keeping, carpentry, smithying, weaving and tannery, and also for hands-on sanitation work in the art and spirit of cooperation.
- To give the students elementary instruction in the sciences connected with their practical work, to train them to think over and observe their findings accurately and to express and record the knowledge acquired by them for their own benefit and for that of their fellow people.

The institute carried out this entire programme at two levels: through its headquarters at Sriniketan by running a number of demonstration and service units from there, and simultaneously in the villages, through its workers who lived and worked in the villages itself. The work involved agricultural projects, animal husbandry, health, education, cottage industries, and village organization under the following units:

Farm

The Sriniketan farm demonstrated to the villagers better methods of cultivation by introducing the use of manure, conservation of moisture, rotation of crops, and the use of better seeds. Attention was also given to improving the condition of the cattle by proper breeding and scientific feeding through growing fodder crops. Proper poultry farming was encouraged for the better production of eggs in the villages.

Rural School

A new school called Siksha-Satra was founded in 1924 'with a few boys' to attend to the problems of rural education. Started in Santiniketan in 1922, the school was moved to Sriniketan in 1924. Originally, the boys admitted were either orphans or came from destitute families who could not have normally sent their children to any school at all. The school's goal was to combine basic studies with practical training in the needs of daily living.

Siksha-Satra had three goals. The first was to give the boys full opportunity to mingle with their natural and social environment and this was why the school was moved from Santiniketan to Sriniketan, where they could have a closer contact with their own cultural life. Second, their learning was to be given through creative occupations related to their daily necessities, such as gardening and craft work. They were thus encouraged to take a greater responsibility in meeting their own daily requirements. Third, their curriculum was designed in such a way that their knowledge of formal subjects would be connected to their basic activities.[52]

Village Welfare

The goal of this department was to extend the activities of the institute to the villages and to encourage self-help among the villagers, so that they could improve their own villages through mutual aid and common endeavour. They were guided to do this by means of economic, educational, and health programmes. Rural surveys were carried out for investigating various aspects of economic life. Rural banks, paddy stores, weavers' cooperatives, and irrigation and health societies were set up with the participation of the villagers. For the senior villagers, training camps were launched in the social services, alongside adult education centres with circulating libraries and lantern lectures to spread information. In healthcare, an outdoor dispensary was started along with supporting advice from doctors and nurses. For the prevention of diseases, anti-malarial measures were taken up, inoculation against small-pox was started, as well as the training of *dai*s or midwives for child delivery. An awareness programme was in place for relief work in case of famines and epidemics. In education, the Brati-Balaka or Scout Movement, a night school for boys, and a day school for girls were started.

Brati-Balakas

Sriniketan started its own Brati-Balaka organization by setting up groups of young boys, adolescents, and young men in each village. The goal was that these groups would identify the specific problems and difficulties faced by the villages and help with resolving the problems as and when needed. The idea also was to stir the boys and the men into taking action on their own. It was hoped that the overall effort would contribute to the work of rural reconstruction in the long run. The Brati-Balakas went to camps annually and were given training in the various aspects of everyday living as well as in ways to tackle their recurring problems. This included clearing jungles in their own villages, participating in door-to-door anti-malarial measures, attending village sanitary camps, participating in games, learning handicraft, songs and drama, and participating in famine relief. The arrangement was so structured that the Brati-Balaka organization could work as a parallel centre of education. By 1928, there were 30 centres of Brati-Balaka associations with 800 members.

Rural Industries

Traditional crafts was once upon a time a thriving industry in some of the villages of Birbhum. But this too went into decline along with the general decline of the villages. One of the initiatives of the institute was to revive the weaving culture of the past. There were as many as 6,000 weavers and 20,000 *muchi*s or tanners in Birbhum, but they had lost their skills due to neglect and disorganization over the years. They had to therefore relearn their own traditional craft, and also get training in the modern techniques of production and marketing, so that the revival could serve as a source of income for the villagers. One of the early steps taken at Sriniketan was to set up a crafts education centre, named Silpa-Bhavana, to carry out this reorganization by starting training schemes in new techniques for the local artisans with the goal of making their products financially viable.

Economic Improvement and Cooperatives

The Visva-Bharati Central Cooperative Bank was established in 1927. Its jurisdiction covered an area of 300 square miles and a population of two lakhs. Overall, 200 cooperative societies were launched in the spheres of agricultural credit, irrigation, and also for running the granaries. These were part of Sriniketan's 'Extensive' programmes. One-tenth of that area or 35 square miles, which covered 12 villages, was taken up for the 'Comprehensive' programme of rural reconstruction. The Comprehensive programme was structured under the heads of Health, Education, Economic Improvement, and

Social Work. Economic improvement was sought through setting up cooperatives and extending industries. Two enterprises deserve special mention in this regard. One was the starting of a weavers' cooperative during 1933–35, with the stated objective of making their business financially independent of Sriniketan in the course of time. The other was to give 'training to the Bayens of Bahadurpur in shoemaking and improving their economic condition'.[53]

Social Work, Rural Recreation, and Festivals

Social activity was centred around holding weekly Hari Sabhas and also reading groups for adults. Village festivals were revived with organizing *jatra*s, kirtans, bhajans, and *kathaka*s. Temples and mosques were repaired. Rabindranath never lost an opportunity to encourage the village reconstruction team to find an appropriate place for the arts, for stirring the poet and the artist in each individual, and thereby, uplifting their human emotions. The traditional festivals were held regularly at Sriniketan, like the festivals to celebrate the seasons. Dramas and musical programmes were organized on many occasions. Rabindranath wrote a plethora of songs and dramas for the seasons, which were presented at the Santiniketan and Sriniketan school festivals.

Two important festivals were held regularly in Sriniketan itself. One was a village fair with an exhibition of Sriniketan's products, vegetables and fruits, plants and handicrafts. That was held in February at the annual Maghotsav celebration, which was also the institute's Foundation Day. The other was the Halakarshan, or the ploughing festival, held in the rainy season. Rabindranath used to encourage the leading Kala-Bhavana artist, Nandalal Bose, to mingle with the village craftspersons in creating new and original designs for the festival entry gates. Elmhirst wrote about Rabindranath:

> From the earliest days he would urge us to draw upon all the resources, in music, song, drama and dance, drawing and design, at Santiniketan in order to enrich our lives, to liven our aspirations, to inspire our leisure and to increase our delights in every kind of artistic expression. He was not happy until we and the cultivators could produce a richness and a wealth of cultural life of our own, and a rejuvenation of those ancient art-forms that still survived, but only so tenuously, in the villages around us.[54]

It is evident from some of the contemporary accounts that there were many negative results at the start of the Sriniketan scheme of rural reconstruction. That was only understandable, given that the funds were limited and the staff were mostly untrained. Rabindranath's objective of the many-sided approach to village reconstruction, so that all aspects of the individual could be included, was not easy to fulfill. But from our study of the records, we can legitimately conclude that the early workers were exemplary in their willingness to face the problems squarely, to learn from their adverse experiences, and not ever easily give up. There was complete transparency over their successes and failures. That is how the work was sustained even with its ups and downs. The flag was kept flying, which we can well feel from what Rabindranath wrote to Elmhirst: 'You know my heart is with Surul. I feel that it has life in it—it does not deal with abstractions, but has its roots deep in the heart of living reality. You may be absolutely certain that it will be able to weather all storms and spread its branches wide.'[55]

To that Elmhirst replied, equally spiritedly: 'You are right about Surul. I think I can understand something of what a mother can feel for her child now. It has taken of my very life's blood, and as I read over all my messages from the other side of the world again, I felt its call.'[56]

Agriculture and Industries at Sriniketan

> It has been my earnest desire for long that we in this country should deal with the problems of agriculture in a big way. I had sent some of our young men abroad to study agriculture, so that on their return home they might tackle this problem and thus serve their motherland. During those days I had said in my article 'Swadeshi Samaj' that we have to reconstruct our national life with the village at the centre.[57]

The Sriniketan scheme of rural reconstruction was initially named the Department of Agriculture, Santiniketan. With agriculture being the main occupation of the rural people, it was given the first place. A complete plan of agricultural work by scientific and improved methods of agriculture was drawn up from the beginning. This included experiments with seeds, manures, rotation of crops, cattle breeding, and poultry farming. A fundamental objective was to reduce the poverty of the villager and also to cut down on their hard labour. Most of the farmers practised primitive methods of cultivation. What was needed was to introduce methods for conservation of the land and to develop water resources, what was scientifically known as 'conservation farming'. It was also thought necessary to revamp the village administration by working 'with' the farmers to induce a greater degree of enthusiasm among the farmers for the improvements that were being attempted.

An integrated plan was made for the cropping system, so that the rotation of crops would include legumes and fruit trees accompanied by following the principles for soil conservation and the maintenance of soil fertility. It was assumed that all those factors would be linked to the people's financial and nutritional needs, and consequently, to create an improvement in the villagers' standard of living. It was hoped that the people's interest in improvement could be harnessed for the effective execution of the 'integrated' plan. The area chosen for the integrated plan of an all-round scheme of development along with the application of science to the rural problems, mainly in respect of agriculture, was 10,000 acres. This area included 22 villages in the district of Birbhum with Sriniketan as the headquarters.

The overall goal at all the levels remained consistent with Sriniketan's foundations, which was to win the friendship and affection of the villagers by making an honest effort to understand their concerns and to see how best to solve their most pressing problems. The other goal was research and experiment, whereby experts would be invited to Sriniketan to serve as a laboratory in combining the new scientific knowledge with the traditional experiences of the villagers. These experiments aimed at finding better methods of growing crops, growing vegetables, obtaining credit, selling their produce to their best advantage, buying their requirements to their best advantage, such as the use of improved tools which the peasants could afford. Alongside, a training programme was launched for apprentices who were intending to take up farming as their vocation.

It was understood that the inbuilt deficiencies in rural agriculture, which hindered its improvement and overall growth, could not be resolved. These deficiencies lay in the small and fragmented holdings as well as in the system of tenancy which provided no rights to the land. Those deficiencies were beyond Sriniketan's control to change.

Therefore, what Sriniketan was attempting to change were some of the other causes that hindered improvement of rural agriculture, such as addressing the issues of ignorance, illiteracy, antiquated methods of tilling, inability to buy improved tools, and poorly groomed bullocks. An example is on record in what Elmhirst wrote about his own direct experience with the village plough: 'I took a hand with the local one-handed plough, an antique weapon which does no turning over of the soil, but drives a spike down into it about five inches deep, like the spike of a harrow.'[58]

What was new in the institute's agricultural programme was that they introduced vegetable gardening in every village family, so as to improve their health through a better diet without any additional cost. The Japanese gardener, Kasahara, was given charge of the fruit and vegetable garden. All kinds of vegetables were grown on a plot of land, which came to be known as 'the Kasahara garden'. A contemporary colleague at Sriniketan, Prem Chand Lal, who joined the Sriniketan Institute as Deputy Director in 1923, wrote the following appreciation about Kasahara:

> He [Kasahara] was a perfect example of industry and hard work, and succeeded in raising all kinds of vegetables on a piece of land declared by agricultural experts to be absolutely unfit for growing vegetables. People from long distances came to see his garden, and were amazed at the beautiful crops and large variety of Indian, English, Japanese and Chinese vegetables grown by him.[59]

The Sriniketan team thought it best to demonstrate to the farmers what could be done to apply improved and scientific methods even on a limited scale in their own farming. They were shown how this could be done by experimentation and research. One other example was the cultivation of green-manuring crops. The team also tried to help the farmers with certain practical problems, such as that of storage. The farmers grew potatoes wherever there was good irrigation, but they did not know where and how to store a large harvest of potatoes. A new method was introduced by the Surul Department of Agriculture for the storage of potatoes which the farmers could afford. Even though it was the institute's goal to make all the productive units economically self-sufficient, that was mostly not possible.

Another important factor that hindered the improvement of agriculture lay in the declining condition of the dairy department. There was a scarcity of fodder with the result that the cattle were undernourished. Healthy cattle-breeding was a fundamental need in agriculture. One of the targets of the Sriniketan Institute, therefore, was to breed cattle not only at its dairy farm, but also to get the individual cultivators to breed cattle by using the scientific methods to get not only good milch cows, but also hardy draught animals.

A revolutionary move taken by the Sriniketan experiment was in the inclusion of cottage industries as an essential part of the programme for rural reconstruction. As agriculture could not be the only source of sustenance, given how dependent it was on the elemental forces, and considering how dependent the Birbhum farmers were on the sole rice crop, it was almost essential to have an alternative source of production. The Arts were a vital resource for the Sriniketan experiment as we have noted in the Introduction. The need to give creative expression to human being's natural emotional responses was essential to Santiniketan's and Sriniketan's way of life. The idea was to appeal to the natural artist in each individual through drama, dance, and music. By the same token, attention was given to creativity in design. Rabindranath encouraged the artists of Santiniketan's Kala-

Bhavana to cooperate with the village weavers and potters in creating new designs for the objects of everyday use. He was known to have said, 'Invite our artist Nandalal to meet the village craftsmen. He may stimulate them into producing new and original designs.'[60]

Another feature of this movement for innovation in the arts was in the making of indigenous dyes. This was taken up as a subject of research between Santiniketan and Sriniketan. It became commercially successful. Here is a report from the venture itself:

> Research in indigenous dyes and in new patterns is carried on as much as time permits, and the results are tried out at the Institute before taking them to the weavers or for teaching the apprentices. Commercially, this section has quite justified its existence. Allowing for the time the instructors spend in the educational and extension work, it has been found to be one of the best paying options. According to the Report of the Institute for the year 1929, there were 214 students in the Weaving Section alone from various backgrounds who had received training in making the dyes. Some of them were weavers and some were schoolteachers. By improving their designs and from working on improved looms, the weavers increased their income considerably. Several among them who were not weavers by caste went through the cooperative marketing process for the sale of their products. But those who took to this trade, made a much better living than they did earlier.[61]

There was a wide spectrum of industries that the Sriniketan programme of rural reconstruction encouraged and supported. These were weaving, tannery, carpentry, lacquer craft, pottery, bookbinding, embroidery, and tailoring. There was also a mechanical workshop. All these industries were brought under Sriniketan's Silpa-Bhavana and were guided by its members. Among them, weaving and tannery were doing well; the others were not as commercially successful. Earlier, there were 3,600 leather workers in the district. As with the weavers, earlier the leather craft too had gone into decline. It was for its revival that Sriniketan's tannery was started as an experiment in 1924. During the years from 1924 to 1930, several *muchis*, who were leather workers by caste, were trained at Sriniketan. An apprentice of the tannery section was sent to the Calcutta Research Tannery to learn bark-tanning. He returned to work at Sriniketan after finishing his training. The leather industry made artistic leather products, like handbags, cushion covers, portfolios, and leather stools or *moras* filled with straw. Another tannery project was launched to give training to the *bayens* of Bahadurpur in shoemaking and improving their economic condition. The goal was to turn this project into a cooperative 'after a period when a fair market will be created for the products'. There was a plan to include other villages for the same project after Bahadurpur.[62]

The lacquer industry was also taken up for revival. There was a time when Birbhum's Ilambazar town was well known for its lacquer work. An estimated number of 60 families were engaged in this work then. That effort too went into decline when the workers were stricken by malaria and kala-azar. Sriniketan tried a revival strategy by persuading two of those families to produce artistic leather goods. That is how Sriniketan's artistic crafts in leather, cloth, and wood helped to transform the taste of Bengal and other parts of the country.

Carpentry was also started under the charge of an expert who received his training in Sweden. He was Lakshmiswar Sinha (1905–1977, crafts teacher and cabinet-maker), who created a steady flow of high quality furniture with innovative designs in the 1930s. He came to work for the Sriniketan Institute of Rural Reconstruction in 1923 and, at first, learned woodwork from Kasahara. Later, he became a crafts teacher at the Santiniketan school and was sent to Sweden in 1928 to train in the Swedish Sloyd Method of furniture-making. Most of the furniture he made catered to the local Santiniketan and Sriniketan communities, as it was not feasible to sell these in the Calcutta market due to the high cost of transportation.[63]

There was often a dilemma in Visva-Bharati's inner circles as to whether Sriniketan's artistic products should adopt a 'business model' rather than remain mainly as a centre for creative design. The economist, Sudhir Sen, who came to work for Sriniketan in the late 1930s, the author of *Rabindranath Tagore on Rural Reconstruction* (1943), had brought this matter up with Rathi Babu. He proposed to make Santiniketan's and Sriniketan's artistic products into a marketable endeavour, instead of using them as a purely artistic endeavour as art for art's sake. While Rathi Babu agreed that 'commercial success' was a necessity, he explained that an institution like Visva-Bharati had an obligation to experiment with new designs and thus contribute to the world of art.[64]

It was fundamentally Rabindranath's idea, and his exceptional prescience, to supplement the villagers' agricultural activity with cottage industries. He thought of this early on, while living and working with the tenant farmers in his family's agricultural estates. In 1911–12, he wrote a telling letter from the Patisar estate to Rathi on the subject of bringing cottage industry to the life of the farmer and making it a cooperative business proposition. He wrote:

> A rice mill has been working at Bolpur. A similar mill would be very useful here [Patisar]. This is pre-eminently a paddy growing tract and it grows more paddy than the Bolpur area.

I think a solid beginning in cooperative work can be made if the cultivators were to run a mill collectively with ownership distributed among themselves in the form of five-rupee or ten-rupee shares. With advances from our bank, this business of rice milling could easily be established here. Both Nagendra (Nagendra Nath Ganguli), and Janaki (estate staff), think that this enterprise would suit this region and benefit the tenants. Do be on the lookout for such a mill.

I was also thinking of what industries would be best suitable for the cultivators of this locality. Nothing grows here except paddy. The only other thing they possess is hard clay. I want to know if pottery can be introduced here as a cottage industry. Will you find out if the people of a village can collectively run such an industry with the help of a small furnace? It would be useful if they could manufacture rough plates and cups like the '*sanki*' pottery used by the Muslim communities in their daily life.

There is yet another possibility, namely, umbrella-making. If we could get hold of a suitable person to give the necessary training, we can use this craft in the Selidaha region.

Nagendra was telling me that it would be of great advantage if we could bring over a potter here who could make tiles. People are keen on tin-roofs, but cannot afford them. Tiles would be a welcome substitute.

In any case, do enquire about the rice-mill, the wheel for pottery, and an expert for umbrella-making.

I am going to inspect the Ratwal region tomorrow. From there, we shall visit Kamta and then shall start for Selidaha, perhaps on Thursday next.[65]

The Village Welfare Department, Sriniketan

> The life of India is in her villages, and the greatest need of the country is village reconstruction. Sriniketan is making a definite and co-ordinated attempt to bring back life in its completeness into the villages. The task before us today is to make whole the broken-up communal life, to harmonise the divergence between village and town, between the classes and the masses, between the pride of power and the spirit of comradeship. We must see that a force from within the people starts functioning.[66]

It was recognized early in Sriniketan's work of rural reconstruction that gathering statistics and organizing rural surveys would have to be among the basic tools for collecting information about the villages for taking the work forward. The Department of Village Welfare was entrusted with the task of formulating and instituting rural surveys. The department was also given charge of the Brati-Balaka organizations, girls' school, night school, training camps for social workers, circulating libraries, and lantern lectures. In addition, they had to administer the dispensary and take measures for the control of malaria, other epidemics, and also fire and famine relief work.

Of these, the most difficult to achieve was health care for the villagers. Elmhirst wrote in his Sriniketan diary on 19 June 1922:

> Ploughing from 6 to 8, bandaged patients, and tried out the new doctor till 11 p.m. and had a feeling from his arrival that he would never do for us. As soon as I saw how [badly] he treated the little Santal girl who caught her finger in the roller and nearly took the top right off. I realized that for him she was not a human being at all, nor were the Mahidapur farmers, just so many animals. I could see him driving them away with his rudeness and rough handling. 'But why should I treat them at all?' he said to me. 'They are not labourers in your employ. Send them to the hospital.' When he said he was already married I knew he would never settle out here in the wilds.[67]

We know from the earlier chapters that it was proving difficult to get the services of a professional doctor who would treat the villager considerately and not contemptuously. Not succeeding in that ideal immediately, Elmhirst arranged through Dorothy Straight for a paramedical professional from New York to join the work and set up a clinic at Sriniketan in 1923.[68] This was Miss Gretchen Green. The Village Welfare Department did all they could to carry out the Health work with qualified medical staff. After some time, a medical officer was given the authority to steer this programme. According to the institute's Annual Report of 1929, there were 6,760 patients treated at the departmental dispensary. There was further progress when the Village Welfare Department under Kalimohan Ghose's leadership set up cooperative health societies in the villages, within a range of approximately 10 miles or more between the villages.

Treatment at the dispensary was not entirely free. The doctor did not have to be paid, but the patients had to pay the price of medicines. Members of the health cooperatives got the medicines at a discount, not the non-members. That was a way of incentivizing more people to take membership to the health societies. The poor and the destitute were of course treated completely free. The medical staff would visit the individual patient who was too ill to come to the dispensary. The medical team was assisted by the Brati-Balakas or the scouts for collecting data on malaria in each village and also when there were cases of cholera. They were given the task of distributing quinine to the malaria patients.[69]

The other significant health work that the institute tried to establish was the practice of midwifery. It was very difficult to find women doctors to come and live and work in the villages, more than finding male doctors. The idea, therefore, was to substitute a lady doctor by the midwife appointed by the Sriniketan institute. The maternity cases were attended by the midwives, who also gave classes in the villages on maternity, nursing, health, hygiene, and childcare. There were also the traditional village midwives, the *dai*s. They were called in to take further training from the midwifery classes and from the lecture demonstrations on hygiene and sanitation. The midwives were, in addition, entrusted to form women's cooperative societies in the villages. Being accomplished in embroidery and sewing, the midwives taught these skills to the schoolgirls.[70]

The institute's goal was to attract villagers to a better way of life by getting them to attend the lectures for all. Most of the lectures were given by the institute's staff, though, occasionally, guests were invited to give lectures. Speakers also came from Santiniketan. Lectures were given on health and hygiene, particularly on the prevention of malaria and cholera, which were the two common ailments in the villages. The other topics for the lectures were cooperation, religious toleration, festivals, and some cultural aspects of community living.

Twenty-six such lectures were given in the year 1929, according to the year's annual report. As many as 19 villages were included for the roving lectures and attended by approximately 6,000 villagers. Besides arranging those standalone lectures, the Village Welfare Department also organized training camps. A circulating library was moreover started by the Village Welfare Department. At the beginning, 15 villages were covered by the circulating library, which distributed or issued 729 books. This was another important contribution to the cause of education in the villages.[71]

The circulating library was also used by the schools, which were administered by the Village Welfare Department. Girl's and women's education was given priority. A girl's school in Sriniketan's neighbouring village grew from strength to strength. The girls came from all castes and were admitted without discrimination. From the very beginning, the girls were taught some special craft, something which they could hold in their small hands, and which was of some definite economic value to them. The literacy side was also included, such as learning the three 'R's (reading, writing, and arithmetic). But the main effort was to establish a closer connection between school studies and daily life experience. To that effect, they were taught needlework, embroidery, cooking, and gardening. Two teachers were engaged for the girls' school. There was provision for the girls to participate in the outdoor games, like badminton. We will discuss more about Sriniketan's elaborate education programme in a chapter specifically dedicated to the subject.

As mentioned earlier, the Scout Movement was felt to be of utmost importance to Sriniketan's first director, L.K. Elmhirst, who introduced it among the village boys in 1923. It was named the 'Sahayak Sangha' at its inception. The programme was brought under Elmhirst's direct leadership and had received Rabindranath's blessings. Initially, the organization included students from the primary school as well as the older boys. Their programme of work included games, drill, tree-climbing, swimming, reading, nature study, collecting specimens, story-telling, music, and drama performances, drawing and painting, and any one of the cottage industries from a choice of weaving, basket-making, mat-making, carpentry, and pottery. Their training also included the social service activities of the Village Welfare Department. The idea was that there would be an opportunity in the future for such boys and girls to play a major role in the villages after receiving an all-round system of elementary education that was being built on the villagers' own need to grow, to imagine, and to explore.[72]

In 1921, four students were sent from the institute to the Central Provinces on a training programme in the organization of Scout troops. From then on, they became the Brati-Balaka Organization. They were divided into three sections, Brati-Dal, Brati-Balaka, and Yuva-Sangha. The senior group belonged to the age group of 12–14, the junior group were admitted up to age 11, and the youth consisted of those above 14. They were guided by a scout leader from the institute. This was done with the help and support of the headmaster of the village school, who proved to be an asset to Sriniketan's Scout Movement in those early days.

The Brati-Balaka ideal we know was for 'cooperative action' and 'obedience' in cooperative action. Group games played an important role in achieving this ideal. With this background, they were trained to give public service in the form of supervising sanitation and policing of the crowded village fairs. Other barriers of social customs were broken down in the process, such as giving service with their hands for any work that needed to be done. We have P.C. Lal's account of this successful aspect of Sriniketan's Brati-Balaka Organization during the 1930s:

> The experiment was so successful that afterwards the institute undertook similar work (of social service) at all the fairs of the locality, and especially at the one held at Kenduli, a place about 18 miles from Sriniketan, and the biggest fair in the

> district. Kenduli is the birthplace of Jaya Deva, the founder of the Vaishnavite Sect in Bengal. The fair lasts about five days and is visited by nearly 50,000 pilgrims, coming from all parts of Bengal, some coming from outside the province. It is known all over North India. Under the leadership of our scout leader, and the village, every year about thirty to forty scouts from the institute and from the neighbouring villages are taken to this fair, to look after the sanitation and policing work. After the first year, the chairman of the District Board deputed a physician to work under our direction, and also contributed a certain sum of money towards the expenses. The 'mahant' (chief priest) of the temple also recognized the value of our services, and agreed to provide the whole party with free rations, while from the pilgrims themselves, we received nothing but gratitude and admiration.[73]

Stirring the villagers to action and to equip them to meet the challenges of the future society was one of the primary objectives for rural reconstruction. Realizing that the older villagers were indifferent to the change being initiated, the Scout Movement became a potential and successful resource. There were two approaches of forming the Brati-Balaka troops, those that were formed by the participating schools and organized by the school's teaching staff from among the schoolboys. The other approach was to collect them from the non-schoolgoing children and to mobilize them in separate troops on a regional basis. As more and more schools developed the extracurricular activities, social, emotional, and vocational, the Brati Movement came to prominence in its different locations.

It would be interesting to note that the second full-time director of the Sriniketan Institute, after Leonard Elmhirst, was a former

Brati-Nayak. He was Dhirananda Ray (1902–1971), who joined the Sriniketan Institute in 1922, and was sent to train as a Brati-Balaka, where he did very well. After returning from training, he was offered the position of the Chief Brati Organizer from 1923. This is what he wrote of his experience of the Brati organization in 1936: 'Brati-Balaka work, practically speaking, was my life's work. In 1923, it was started with 20 boys only, and now, after continuous and strenuous efforts, this organization has stood on a sound basis with 400 boys. So long I had no other thought, but of Brati-Balakas.'[74]

A remarkable feature of the Brati Movement was how it became the basis also for enhancing the artistic life of the villages. To fulfill that idea, Rathi Babu, who was in the leadership of Sriniketan overall, picked upon one of Kala Bhavana's art students, Vinayak Shivram Masoji (1897–1977), specifically to join the Brati-Balaka troop for taking art to the villages and for encouraging art activity among the villagers. Rathi Babu wrote about the unique concept as follows:

> I have secured the services of Masoji, who went with Dhira for scout training. I want him to devote himself in finding out and developing the artistic resources of the villages. I shall place him directly under Nandalal Bose to work under his guidance and direction. He will also be able to help Protima in the work she wishes to undertake amongst the women. Protima has brought an oven from Germany and would be setting up a potter's workshop [at Sriniketan] on her return from the hills.[75]

The Village Welfare Department was entrusted with carrying out the village festivals, among which there were the Maghotsav and Halakarshan, Nababarsha or the Bengali new year, Barsha Mangal for celebrating the rainy season, Briksharopan for tree planting, Basantotsav for celebrating the season of spring, Nabanna for celebrating the harvest, and Silpotsav for showcasing the rural crafts and industries. At Silpotsav, there was a display of the equipment used by the artisans. While being joyous, the festivals were also utilitarian in purpose. The overall aim was to replenish and restore the environment and that was especially true of the idea of Briksharopan, the tree-planting festival, about which Rabindranath wrote:

> The situation seems very much like what it was in the early period of the Earth when she ceaselessly underwent the fiery ordeal of forging and hammering and a ruthlessness that seemed like the anarchy of an unmeaning topsyturvydom. Man's greed grew as he received Mother Earth's bounty. That greed led to the denudation of forests in favour of agricultural land. Men cut down trees to meet their endless needs and stripped the Earth of shade. As a result, the air became increasingly hotter, while the fertility of the soil alarmingly diminished. That is how, northern India, deprived of its shelter of forests, now lies scorched by the harsh rays of the sun. With all this in our minds, we initiated a tree-planting ceremony to teach the children to replenish the plundered stores of Mother Earth.[76]

What is significant to note is that the village festivals were organized by using only local resources, so that they would not be expensive. A local person like the village headman was asked to steer the festival as its leader and a local team was asked to stage the show. Only local flowers were used to decorate the precincts. Rabindranath's instructions were to make use of the 'fallen leaves' if flowers were not available. He also asked for the decoration to be kept very simple and natural and to stage the show in the open, preferably underneath a tree, and not try for anything artificial like putting up a stage. The idea was to engage with participation from the grassroot level, and to identify local leadership, to discover local talent to encourage group activity. About this important aspect of village regeneration in the Sriniketan experiment, the author of *A Poet and A Plan* expressed the following view from his field research on the subject. He wrote, 'The festivals were indeed made the vehicles through which some of the major objectives of rural development could be brought home to the participating community. They represented a process of total enlivenment of the participating rural groups, so that their contribution to the whole programme of development could be vigorous, all embracive, spontaneous, and self-helpful.'[77]

The ideal was to raise the village morale from the humiliation of 'being' on perpetual charity. Rabindranath's urge was to bring joy, music, and festivity to the villages even if that was possible in just a very few villages. His hope was to establish the ideal, so that it could take root with time. Here below is what he said to a group of writers, musicians, and artists, who were visiting Sriniketan in 1936:

> The picture of the helpless village which I saw each day as I sailed past on the river has remained with me and so I have come to make the great initiation here. It is not the work for one, it must involve all. I have invited you today not to discuss my literature nor listen to my poetry. I want you to see for yourself where our society's real work lies. That is the reason why I am pointing to it over and over again. My reward will be if you can feel for yourself the value of this work.[78]

Siksha-Satra and Other Educational Institutions

> It is well known that the education which is prevalent in our country is extremely meagre in the spread of its area and barren in its quality. Outside the 'bhadralok' class pathetic in its struggle to affix university labels to the names of its members, there is a vast obscure multitude who cannot even dream of such a costly ambition. With them, we have our best opportunity if we know how to use it there, and there only can we be free to offer to our country the best kind of all-round culture not mutilated by the official dictators. I have generally noticed that when the charitably minded city-bred politicians talk of education for the village folk they mean a little left over in the bottom of their cup after diluting it copiously. They are callously unmindful of the fact that the kind and amount of food that is needful for the mental nourishment must not be apportioned differently according to the social status of those who receive it.[79]

Education became an important part of the Sriniketan initiative from the very first decade of its existence. There were different levels at which education was imparted. The Sriniketan Institute offered 'extension services' at the adult level of research and experiment.

There were also three separate institutions of education in Sriniketan itself, which were: Siksha-Satra for the village boys, the Loka-Siksha Samsad for the village householders, and the Siksha-Charcha Bhavana for the village school teachers. Dhirendra Mohan Sen (1901–1987), who joined Santiniketan's and Sriniketan's educational work in 1930, wrote this about Rabindranath's engagement with the work: 'Gurudev is taking an active part both in Sriniketan and Santiniketan. He is meeting students and staff often and telling them what he expects of them.'[80]

Siksha-Satra was conceived as a parallel school for the village boys. Its leader Santosh Chandra Majumder worked under the active guidance of Rabindranath and Elmhirst. Santosh Chandra Majumder himself had been an early student of the Santiniketan school. Later, he became a teacher there. In 1924, he took charge of Siksha-Satra, but died prematurely in 1926, when he was only 41. As a result, Siksha-Satra was moved from Santiniketan to Sriniketan in 1926.[81]

Conceptualizing Siksha-Satra was a natural outcome of some years of the educational experiment at Santiniketan. There was also two years of the Sriniketan experience by the time Siksha-Satra was started. It was decided to spare the village boys from the burden of academic courses. That was essential for the pupils of the Santiniketan school who came from urban backgrounds and whose goal was to build professional careers. The Siksha-Satra was conceived as a parallel school for village boys, later also joined by the girls. In Siksha-Satra's curriculum, the students had to devote only one hour to the three 'R's, that is, reading, writing, and arithmetic. As for the rest of the curriculum, the Siksha-Satra boys and girls did nature studies directly from their surroundings. They collected medical herbs, learned gardening, carpentry, painting, cooking, and housecraft. They also learned the rules of maintaining good health. Every Siksha-Satra student had to apprentice himself in some handicraft and housecraft. Elmhirst wrote about the Siksha-Satra student's training programme as follows:

> Under the term housecraft, at the Siksha-Satra, the following functions were treated as of primary educational importance: care and cleaning and construction of quarters; care and proper use of latrines; sanitary disposal of waste; cooking and serving of food; clothes washing and repair; personal hygiene and healthy habits; individual self-discipline; group self-government; policing and hospitality; fire drill and control. In every one of these, there was some art to be mastered, some business or organizing capacity to be developed, some law of science to be recognized, and in all of them there is a call for the recognition of the need for individual self-preservation as well as of the duties, responsibilities and privileges of family membership and citizenship.[82]

Their schooling was initially free, including boarding, lodging, and tuition. At that rate, only 20 boys could be educated in the first decade of the school. By then, some of the senior boys had become expert weavers and carpenters, and it was decided to pay them daily wages for their work, so as to initiate them on the path to self-reliance. From then on, the whole amount due to every student for his productive work was paid to him at the end of the month, from which he was expected to pay for his own tuition and board.

Among the first batch of these boys who completed the Siksha-Satra course, there were some who made good careers. Jnanendranath Ghosh of village Laldaha became an organizer of the Visva-Bharati Central Cooperative Bank, Kalidas Ghosh of village

Jadavpur became a teacher at Siksha-Satra, Badda Hasta of village Bandhlodanga became a teacher in the Santal school, Urugendra Pal of Bogdora became an expert weaver and earned his livelihood by working out of his own loom, and Nandadulal Sutradhar of Ikshudhara, who learned carpentry at Siksha-Satra, returned to his village and prospered in his trade.[83]

Adult Education, Apprenticeships, and Training Camps

The later additions in Sriniketan's educational departments were the Loka-Siksha Samsad of 1936 for Adult Education to educate the householders and the Siksha-Charcha Bhavana of 1937 to train the village schoolteachers. Teaching and learning of handicrafts was compulsory in each of these institutions. Moreover, the Sriniketan authorities invited apprentices from the villages to be attached to different departments of the village organization for a year or more on stipends of 20 rupees each. The departments were Agriculture, Industries, Health, and Sanitation. The length of the apprenticeship at the productive departments depended on the students' earning capacity.[84]

Besides the apprenticeship, arrangements were made for Training Camps where Lantern Lectures were given especially on the topics of causes and prevention of malaria, small pox, cholera, and other common village epidemics.[85] There were extensive discussions on possible ways of economic improvement. It was expected that such gatherings would prepare workers for village reconstruction work. One direct outcome was the spread of the Brati-Balaka troops, which spread to most of the 22 villages which joined the camps. Kalimohan Ghose hosted three such camps in 1924, to which 33 trainees came from 22 villages.[86]

Surveys and Economic Research

Efforts to base village plans on a realistic appraisal of the specific needs of the village, as well as of making realistic statistical estimates by methods of rural survey, came into practice for the Sriniketan programme as early as in 1923. The Department of Economic Research had been included since the institute's inception in 1922. It carried out surveys of the surrounding villages by collecting data that was relevant to programmes of rural reconstruction.

Economic research was classified into three branches, such as agricultural production, economic condition of village families, and an analysis of the villager's 'life' in general, similar to Lal Behari Dey's classic work, *Bengal Peasant Life* (1878). The idea was that the problems of the villages had to be scientifically studied and analyzed, so as to develop enrichment programmes for them. They set about doing this by means of the rural surveys to find out the specific needs of particular villages in the areas of sanitation, medicine, vaccination, prevention against snakebite, maternity work, tanks, irrigation, fishery, poultry, weaving, tanning, education, arbitration, and cooperation with the neighbouring villages. However, within a decade of the Sriniketan work, it was seen that there was a change in the direction of the surveys. They moved from recording facts and figures to drawing conclusions from general principles.

Among the surveys that were published, there were the two early ones by Kalimohan Ghose, namely *Ballavpur* (1926) (see Appendix 1) and *Raipur* (1933). Another such survey, *Supur*, was published in 1940. The other innovative publications in the area of field research was a series called the *Visva-Bharati Rural Studies* and the *Visva-Bharati Economic Research Publications*. The following titles were included in the series: *Three Village Economic Studies on Rice* by Hashim Amir Ali, assisted by Tara Krishna Basu and Jiten Talukdar; *Records of the*

Malaria Survey in Villages in West Bengal by Harry G. Timbres, 1935; *The Savings Bank Movement: Its Origin and Development* by Sudhir Sen, 1938; *Conflict of Economic Ideologies in India* by Sudhir Sen, 1943; and *Land and Its Problems* by Sudhir Sen, 1943.[87]

There were other surveys carried out, which remained unpublished. Some among those were as follows: 'Survey of Rural Indebtedness in South West Birbhum, 1933–44'; 'Rainfall Figures in Bolpur, 1891–1929'; 'Rice Export Figures, Bolpur to E.I. Railway Stations, 1933–40'; 'Size of Holdings, Area of Paddy Lands 1939–40'; 'Crop Costing Statistics and Village Land Statistics, 1939'; 'Enquiry into Land Tenure, 1939–49'; 'Economic Condition of the Bargadars 1941–43'; 'Village Enquiry of Goalpara, 1942–49'; and 'Data Collected from Five Different Villages and Three Santal Bastis, 1932–33'. The latter contained sociological data on five classes—the High Castes, the 'Nabasaktis', the Muslims, the Harijans, and the Santals, as well as economic data on their assets, liabilities, incomes, and expenditures. Some of these were later included in the publication *Then and Now* by Hashim Amir Ali, Tara Krishna Basu, and Jitendranath Talukdar, Calcutta, 1958. Hashim Amir Ali (1903–1987), was an Elmhirst Fellow in Economic Research at Sriniketan from 1931 to 1934. Tara Krishna Basu and Jitendranath Talukdar were his assistants during the same period.

Besides the surveys, one other important approach in reaching the minds of the villagers was through single printed sheets or 'fliers' titled the *Prochar Patromala* (Information Sheets). Many of those were distributed during 1930–41. These were written on the popular topics of the day. Some examples of these were 'Mahuar Chaash', 'Darjeeling Potato', 'Taal Goor', 'Motihari Tobacco', 'Dhaan Chaash er Tothyo Sangroho, 1941–44', 'Grambasi der Tothyo Sangroho, 1941–56'.

Other projects included publications on 'Cottage Craft in Supur', 1939, which were printed reports on the project for making fans with palmyra leaf and on 'Spinning and Weaving in Supur', 1939; 'Sanai Music in Supur', 1939; 'All-Sided Development of the Santal Colonies 1934'; 'Brati-Balaka Activities', 1923–31, 1938, 1941, 1942; 'Brati-Balaka Rally 1938–42'; 'Brati-Balaka Organisation 1937–43', 'Brati-Balaka Numerical Strength 1934'; 'Brati-Balaka List of Local Troops, 1923–31'; 'Weekly Reports' by Chief Brati-Balaka Organiser, 1940, 1941, 1942.[88]

The institute at Sriniketan served principally as the laboratory, where experiments for the reconstruction of villages were carried out. The goal was not always to find the solution of a problem, but more to explore how the problem could be understood and tackled. There is no denying that a considerable amount of work was undertaken by Sriniketan even with its limited resources. The thrust and the ideal of this institute was that the rural problems had to be approached from all fronts—health and education, economic improvement, and social and cultural activity.

Anti-Malaria Research and Cooperative Health Societies

> As our experience of the problems grew, so did our need for specialist help and advice. Dr. Harry Timbres, an American Quaker, volunteered to do fundamental research into the life, habits, and control of the malarial mosquito. There was no DDT in those days, but year by year the incidence of malaria in the area fell in the face of a well-planned campaign.
>
> The struggle to achieve willing cooperation in simple ways, not involving money, was a long one. Faith in cooperative credit or money schemes had been in some measure destroyed before we arrived; so that it was a long time before the capacity of mutual trust developed to a stage where monetary contributions could be pooled and used for a common purpose, such as a health society.[89]

It became very obvious at the beginning of Sriniketan's work of rural reform that help with health was the quickest way of touching the villager's heart. The villager's health was in shambles. Village life in entirety was infested by malaria, as a result of which, the index of damaged spleens was recorded to be as high as 80 per cent in most of the villages. Nearly everyone who went to live at Surul came down with a malignant fever, especially at the end of the monsoon rains. Santiniketan was comparatively safe, because it stood on a raised ground of sand. Its soil differed entirely from that of Surul, which was on the alluvial mud soil of the Ganges Valley delta. There, even the heaviest monsoon rains would dry off in a few hours. So, it was possible to conduct a great part of the anti-malarial campaign in the earliest days of the experiment from Santiniketan, even though there were also those who had to live in Surul all the year round, right from the start of rural reconstruction. There were millions of deaths every year from malaria, and 10 times that number in case of those who lived in an unfit state of health, and in no condition for manual labour. The malaria problem thus became the gravest of all agricultural issues in the whole of India. As many as one in every four of the Indian population suffered from weak health, according to the prevailing data of those years. This was the same in the villages of West Bengal, and more so, in the district of Birbhum.

The work launched by the Sriniketan team saw to it that little by little, the thick undergrowth was cleared away, the great tank was cleaned, and new houses were built. Gradual changes were brought about to the extent possible. Early on, Kalimohan Ghose took forward the idea of setting up health cooperatives in the villages surrounding the Sriniketan Institute. The method and approach adopted for the health cooperatives followed the terms of the Anti-Malarial Cooperative Society of Bengal.

Sriniketan's first health cooperative was started in the village called Benuria, in 1922. The initiative was taken by calling the villagers to meet and raise subscriptions for a dispensary and a visiting doctor. A house was made available by a leading villager of Benuria to start the Benuria Society. The house, however, got burnt down after some time. After the mishap, the villagers themselves contributed labour, thatch, and cash to build a new house. This was probably evidence that the villagers were benefitting from the cooperative scheme.

Benuria certainly set a good example, though their follow-up work was not as successful.[90]

The health work improved in the 1930s, when the health societies were formalized and spread out to reach an area covering 84 villages and a population of 66,000. The work was further enhanced under the expert leadership of Dr Harry Garland Timbres (1899–1937). A Quaker himself, Dr Timbres was sponsored by the Quaker Organization or the Friends Society of America 'for the work of research and experiment into 'the life, health and control of the malarial mosquitoes.''[91] He and his wife Rebecca came to Santiniketan and Sriniketan in 1931, and stayed till 1934. His remarkable anti-malarial campaign and research work was of the greatest help in serving the villages around Surul. Besides support from The Friends Society, his work was gratefully acknowledged by Mahatma Gandhi who pledged the royalties of three of his books to the anti-malarial campaign undertaken by Dr Harry Timbres.

Timbres unfortunately met with an untimely death. In 1936–37, the couple worked on malaria research in Soviet Russia. It was while they were engaged in that work that he became afflicted with the malaria strain that he was fighting to eradicate and gave his young life to it. He was reputed for his malaria research in the highest scientific circles. Harry and Rebecca Timbres were joint authors of the book titled *We Didn't Ask Utopia,* which was published posthumously in 1970 by Arno Press, New York. Visva-Bharati's Report for 1937 contains the Sriniketan Malaria Team's appreciation and tribute to him in the following words by Rabindranath's closest friend and supporter, Reverend C.F. Andrews (1871–1940):

> All those who are engaged in this wonderful work of recovering the land from the grip of the malaria mosquito

> have asked me to remember this morning with deep affection and esteem Dr. Harry Timbres whose sudden death in Soviet Russia only a short time ago came as a very great shock to us all. We had heard from him in letters how his research work in Surul had been of the greatest help to him in his new work of the same character in Russia where he had gone to help the poor. Our sorrow has been turned into admiration and thanksgiving as we have learnt how he met his death. There, far away, while all too strenuously carrying on his work among the Russian peasants he had contracted dysentery, pneumonia, and typhus fever and in his weak state of health he had no resisting powers. So he died truly a martyr to the cause of Science and the healing of the poor.[92]

The health societies were affiliated to a Health Union, which was located at Sriniketan along with a central hospital and clinic attached to it. The societies worked on both preventive and curative measures of the ailments that were endemic in the villages. What the rural health cooperative worked on was the principle of making the doctor-in-charge responsible for the good health of all the members. The doctor was entrusted with advising and monitoring the patients from time to time. As his income did not depend on the number of patients, but was a fixed monthly salary, he did not have a vested interest in their diseases, rather every interest in their good health.

The village health societies were run on the following lines:

- Producing a detailed study of a village or villages grouped under the particular health society, along with the social and economic condition of their inhabitants, including incidences of the diseases incurred.

- Developing people's awareness about the need for better health through creating and distributing propaganda material.
- Continuing to spread education on health, hygiene, and sanitation through lectures and exhibitions.
- Organizing a medical establishment with a qualified medical officer, a compounder, and a dispensary, to be run on a cooperative basis, with each member paying a subscription in cash or in labour of equal value.
- Arranging for regular health checkup of its members and maintaining the health records of its members.
- Carrying out sanitation and preventive work with organized squads of young men from the villages for filling up stagnant pools, supervising roads and drains, preventing the breeding of mosquitoes, clearing of jungles, and turning waste lands into fruit and vegetable gardens.[93]

Health cooperatives were generally formed with a membership of 200 families. In order to obtain that number, the membership could be extended to other villages. The membership covered the whole family. Contributions were fixed according to the paying capacity of the majority of the residents. In the health societies administered by the Sriniketan Institute, every member paid a subscription of 5 rupees in cash or in labour of equivalent value. There was enough flexibility to allow a member to pay half the subscription in cash and the rest in labour. Those who could not pay any cash could become a member by contributing 16 days of labour in a year. All those who paid their subscription, in cash or by labour, enjoyed the same privileges of a normal membership.

Each cooperative unit had to maintain a dispensary with a qualified doctor and a compounder. Members received medical advice free of charge at the dispensary. A small fee of 4 annas had to be paid, if the doctor was given a call home. Members obtained medicine at cost price. Non-members paid the market price. Non-members also paid the doctor's fee. The income obtained from these collections was credited to the society's funds. It was mandatory for every society to be affiliated to the Health Union. Every society had a Working Committee to which the members elected their office bearers. Only one of the seats was reserved for a nominee of the Health Union. Similarly, the Working Committee sent a representative to the Health Union. The Working Committee's primary charge was to ensure that subscriptions and fees were raised and that the accounts were maintained. The Health Union was in overall charge of each society, including staff appointments to the society or transfers from one society to another, and also dismissals. Each of those had to be approved by the Union.

The Health Union was a central organization, but there were many such health unions. The norm was that any such union would include a group of about 12 contiguous units or cooperatives. Each union maintained a medical officer for supervision and consultation, who would sometimes substitute for a doctor who was absent at an individual unit. The Health Union also maintained a clinic with a nurse and a laboratory technician, a clerk for helping with the records and the accounts, and where possible, depending on its resources, a Publicity Officer. The purpose of a health union was to unite all the health cooperatives, to coordinate their activities, to represent the cooperatives, and to protect their interests in relation to the government and district organizations. They were also empowered to inspect the cooperatives, to audit their records, to purchase the drugs and the materials for the cooperatives, and to promote the formation of more cooperatives.

The Sriniketan Health Union and the cooperatives under its umbrella were an outcome of the 'Intensive' phase of Sriniketan's work, starting from 1933. The Sriniketan Health Union was administered through a dispensary and hospital, a clinical laboratory, the health societies in rural areas, and a maternity and child welfare unit. The villagers were offered medical treatment, anti-malarial sanitation measures, first-aid training to school children, lantern lectures on health propaganda, ante- and post-natal care, training of midwives, and distribution of milk to nursing mothers and babies.[94]

An illustration of the initial Sriniketan effort for health improvement, prior to the Intensive phase, was in village Ballavpur, four miles from Bolpur, which was devastated by malaria. Work had started there as a single unit, in cooperation with the neighbouring villages, much before the later scheme for 'Intensive' and 'Extensive' work was launched. The village worker, Hemanta Sarkar, stayed at Ballavpur from 1928 to 1931. At the time, the idea was to live and work along with the villagers, rather than to work for them from far.[95]

In 1926, a survey of the Ballavpur village was conducted. This classic survey gave the lead to all subsequent work at Ballavpur, according to its specific needs in the spheres of sanitation, medicine, vaccination, maternity work, prevention of snake bite, education, arbitration, banking, gardening, maintenance of tanks for irrigation and fishery, weaving school, tanning, poultry farming, social work of the Rabindra Sevashram, and cooperation with the Santal *basti* or colony and the neighbouring village of Surul.[96]

Ballavpur's progress transformed even the hostile zamindars of the area, such as the Sarkar family, into putting their faith in the goodness of the Sriniketan work of rural reform. They were moved by what they saw, and felt favourably to the Sriniketan experiment for the first time. Earlier, they had given up all hope for Ballavpur's improvement. But they were persuaded to visit the place by their *gomostha,* Sridhar Bhattacharya, who was a long-time resident of Ballavpur. Sriniketan had not only changed the look of the village, but the newly established local branch of the Visva-Bharati Cooperative Bank at Ballavpur gave loans to the cultivators to pay off their arrears to the zamindars. Impressed by the work, the Sarkar family donated a *bigha* of rent-free land to Sriniketan to construct a building for the Ballavpur Rural Reconstruction Society.[97]

The surveys conducted by the health societies were very useful for the future of the villages. The surveys included information under the following heads:

- location of the village
- surroundings
- population
- spleen index
- death rate
- birth rate
- sources of water supply
- manure pits
- latrines
- dwelling houses
- disposal of refuse
- food
- treatment during diseases
- epidemic diseases
- specific diseases
- venereal diseases

Although not all of the village societies were equally successful, the idea as a whole worked quite well. After all, the Sriniketan Institute was a laboratory for experiments on rural reconstruction in the villages, where the foremost idea was to get to know and understand the problem before getting to learn what its solution would be. The health work was one such vital experiment. An examination of the records of the medical work at Surul confirms that malaria had been brought under control. To take an example, the spleen rate in a village near Surul had been brought down from 90 per cent in 1922 to 4 per cent in 1934 and the malarial cases too, from 30 to 1.9 per cent.

Sriniketan in the 1930s: A Changing Scenario

The Silpa-Bhavana Success Story

> I am anxious that steps be taken *without delay* to ensure the presence of business talent in the Councils of Sriniketan.
>
> I can assure you of the cooperation of a few of my near relations at Raipur—only a few because most of the *men* of the family are dead and the few that are there are more or less poor and ignorant—as much in need of help as the rest of the villagers. I say this, only that you may not be under any delusion as to the importance or influence of *the family* at Raipur. In this matter it is only *me* that means Raipur: but to that extent you will have the fullest support from Raipur, *including such financial cooperation as I can afford.*[98]

Thus wrote Lord Satyendra Prasanna Sinha, zamindar and first Baron of Raipur, to Leonard Elmhirst, from their shared concern over the future of the Sriniketan work. Lord Sinha was an eminent barrister and the first Indian to be raised to the peerage and made a member of the Viceroy's Executive Council. He was a close friend of Rabindranath and was of great support to the Sriniketan work, as he was also to Elmhirst. They corresponded and shared their concerns and suggestions for the work. It was becoming evident from the late

1920s that Sriniketan would have to become more business oriented than what had been the case. In the beginning, the foundational thrust of the Sriniketan programme was on research and experimentation, and on guiding the villager to become self-reliant and to grow in *atmashakti*. That early approach began to change from the late 1920s, and progressively during the 1930s.

The change was mainly for Sriniketan to organize marketability for its products, and also to bring about greater overall productivity. The new approach targeted the 'earning departments', that is, those that were among the more productive units. Thus, there was a definite need to look for 'business talent', as Lord Sinha wrote to Elmhirst. The educational units were not per se included in the marketability drive. However, some of those 'earning departments' were concerned with educational value in the sectors where they were linked with industry. In such cases, the district administration was asked to lend some infrastructural support to the Sriniketan Institute and also help with some financial assistance. It was in the context of raising endowments from the government and the private donors that Elmhirst and Lord Sinha were writing to one another. Thus, Lord Sinha wrote again to Elmhirst:

> Keeping in view your very generous promise to continue your grant till 1930, Sriniketan must concentrate, 1stly [sic.] on developing the Departments now existing, 2ndly [sic.] in getting more and more people from the villages to come and *be taught* i.e. shown results; and vigorous propaganda is also necessary for attracting the people, young and old, and 3rdly [sic.], in getting from Govt. and private donors a more or less endowment to the extent of Rs 20,000 or so. I am trying to do what I can, in all 3 ways.[99]

In the 1930s, a promising impact was seen on productivity by the 'new' agriculture that Sriniketan had long been promoting. In that regard, the principal objective had been to increase the productivity of the main crop and to introduce new crops by rotation in the hope of reducing the poverty of the villagers. From the 30s, the changes in this regard were related mainly to the purchasing and marketing side of the concerned enterprises. Adequate purchasing capacity was made mandatory even to apply the cooperative principles for village reform. In other words, progress was tied to the ways and means of improving and increasing production through the method of grading and controlling output to suit market conditions. As we know, the thrust was to spread marketing. The effort was to register every single producer within the marketing organization. That was how the precepts of agricultural economics were introduced and applied for the first time in Sriniketan's work of rural reconstruction.

Rathi Babu drew up a 'reorganization scheme' for Sriniketan in 1934, and again in 1938, both of which emphasized the importance of restructuring Sriniketan 'as a business'.[100] This reorganization scheme announced that the farm, the dairy, and the poultry would be 'leased' out to third parties from 1936 onwards. They would no longer function like 'experimental' research units as was the case in the initial years. Only a two-acre experimental plot of land and two stud bulls were retained for use in the villages. Everything else in the farm, the dairy, and the poultry were leased out.[101] The poultry and the dairy were turned into profit-making production units.

In the course of time, an exercise was carried out to rationalize each and every production unit on business terms.[102] Whenever necessary, funds were diverted to a profit-making unit from a less viable unit. There was once a crisis over diverting the income earned from the weaving section to promote the business of a different unit instead of using it for the welfare of the weavers. The veteran village worker, Hemanta Sarkar, raised a moral issue in the matter and resigned from his job in 1935.[103] Still, rural marketing became a definitive goal in Sriniketan's future work.

It was in this background that Silpa-Bhavana emerged as a success story. Silpa-Bhavana was turned into an independent business unit with a managing board of its own in 1937. It had, of course, played an important role from early on as its initial work had been to revive and support rural crafts. Right from the start, the crafts section was one of the pillars of the Sriniketan experiment of rural reconstruction. As we would know, the traditional handicrafts had been devastated by the Industrial Revolution. Their revival was therefore an ideal in itself from the very beginning of rural reform. By the 1930s, the work of revival came of age and moved on to become a successful business enterprise and a success story at that. Rathi Babu wrote an account about that development. He wrote:

> During a later visit to Europe [in 1930] my wife and myself got ourselves interested in leather work and on our return to the [Santiniketan] asrama many students used to come to learn this interesting work, and the making of fancy articles from leather became the fashion. We took advantage of this and opened a regular workshop for goods. Formerly every bit of leather goods sold in India used to be imported from abroad. As a result of our efforts in training a large number of young men and women, this industry has spread throughout India and already leather goods worth several lacs are being produced in this country.[104]

In the years to come, the attention given to traditional handicrafts led to an important all-India movement through the Handicrafts Board and the All India Cottage Industries Movement. Sriniketan, however, continued to work independently as an institution. The marketing of Sriniketan's beautiful handicrafts brought about a transformation of artistic taste in Bengal and in other parts of India. The art movement of Santiniketan and Sriniketan together brought about a philosophical and practical impact on the reformation of art and craft in modern India. That in itself was a pioneering achievement.

At this time, the weaving section was also making strides. Manindra Chandra Sengupta, who was put in charge of this section, was sent to Japan for training in the running of small scale cotton mills. He brought back with him 10 power looms as well as the accessories that were needed to feed into those machines.[105] Sriniketan's idea of introducing the power loom was to explore if every village could afford to have their own independent mill. The weaving section was exposed to other kinds of looms. Sweden had gifted their model of the handloom to Sriniketan. From it, Sriniketan adopted a 'Swedish' design for curtains, bedcovers, and table cloths. Sriniketan's creation of a 'Swedish' design for its linen became very popular.

What was remarkable about Sriniketan's historic contribution to the revival of the traditional handicrafts with innovative designs was in how it drew young men and women from the surrounding villages to take training in the various handicrafts. They were offered apprenticeships and the incentives offered were free board and lodging for the first few years of an apprenticeship in technical education. What was of further significance lay in the impact of Silpa-Bhavana's business activities on the workers. Between 1938–39 and 1944–45, the number of workers more than doubled from 206 to 525, even though those were the years when the Second World War was raging. We have Rathi Babu writing to Elmhirst about how well Silpa-Bhavana was doing at the time in a letter dated 12 August 1940. He wrote:

> Silpa-Bhavana (Industries department) is steadily improving. The balance sheet of the first quarter just ended shows an all round profit in all the sections. This is the first time that profit and loss accounts have been calculated for each industry, separately. Separate bank accounts are being kept. The total annual sale last year exceeded Rs 50,000/- which is a 40% increase on the previous year. The pottery workshop is emerging from the experimental stage and in order to guarantee a steady supply to the market we are erecting a large oven. Village potters are now sending their biscuit fired wares for glazing at our pottery[sic].[106]

It is crucial to recall that Bengal was overtaken by a terrible famine in 1943 and suffered colossal economic losses. Remarkably, even during that dire situation, Sriniketan kept its doors open for the workers who wanted to work. The table below shows how many workers took up the opportunity.[107] We know from the earlier narrative that Silpa-Bhavana became an independent unit with a managing board of its own from 1937. It could take bold decisions on its own.

TABLE OF NUMBER OF WORKERS	
Year	Workers
1938–39	206
1939–40	217
1940–41	229
1941–42	282
1942–43	325
1943–44	451
1944–45	525

A beneficial feature of the Sriniketan endeavour was that most of the workers associated with the Sriniketan crafts movement worked from their homes. They were not turned into factory workers in any sense of the term. In other words, even when Sriniketan's goods were being manufactured for the market they were not produced on a manufacturing scale as would have been the case with factory owners. In Sriniketan's 'business' model, only 59 of their 525 workers were physically based at the institute. The rest worked from the surrounding villages, independent of the institute, and were paid at a pre-agreed rate based on their monthly turn-out of products. Of the 466 workers who were based in the villages, 244 of them worked directly under Silpa-Bhavana's supervision. They went home at the end of the 6–7 hours of their working day. The others took away the materials from Silpa-Bhavana and worked from their homes. They got paid on delivering their products.

An important feature of the Sriniketan crafts movement was that a 'social' change was becoming quietly discernible among its art and craft workers. The relevant statistics shows how more and more non-caste individuals were joining the work force. The table below for the years 1937–38 to 1944–45 gives us a glimpse of the caste picture.[108]

UNIT-WISE TABLE OF THE CASTE PROFILE		
	Caste Workers	Outside the Caste
Leather work	36	233
Weaving	96	58
Carpentry	7	21
Pottery	2	32

What is also worth observing from the castewise table above is that it was only the weavers who maintained their hold as a hereditary caste group. In other words, the weavers alone came from the weaving community or the weaving caste. It was not so with the leather workers. Leather work was being taken up by 'other' castes as well. There was a comment in the 1947 Bulletin on Silpa-Bhavana, which stated how in leather work the 'better' class of workers belonged to the 'non-professional members', or the non-leather caste. But in the weaving section, the 'better' class of workers belonged to the hereditary weavers community, or those born to the weaver caste. Whether consciously or not, it is worth commenting that Sriniketan's experiment in rural reconstruction was leading to a never-before interface of caste and class. This was relevant because the caste barrier was one of the problems that was present within the workforce itself. The changes coming into play was not only relevant socially and sociologically, but as Rathi Babu wrote, it made it possible to take the rural reform experience to a 'wider field'. In 1938, he wrote to Elmhirst about the benefit of that convergence for the future:

> The time has come to correlate our experiences and work out the methodology of rural reconstruction and devise broader schemes of rural health, rural education, and such vital problems affecting the rural population in conformity with the needs of the country. With the public administration getting more and more autonomous and democratic there is greater interest and a keener demand for carefully worked-out schemes of public welfare. Sriniketan can no longer remain satisfied with meeting the needs of the local rural community—it must begin to think in terms of a wider field.[109]

Some Endemic Problems, Some Tentative Conclusions

> My path, as you know, lies in the domain of quiet integral action and thought, my units must be few and small, and I can but face human problems in relation to some basic village or cultural area. So in the midst of worldwide anguish, and with the problems of over three hundred millions staring us in the face, I stick to my work in Santiniketan and Sriniketan hoping that my efforts will touch the heart of our village neighbours and help them in reasserting themselves in a new social order. If we can give a start to a few villages they would perhaps be an inspiration to some others—and my life work will have been done.[110]

Rabindranath wrote this to Elmhirst from Santiniketan on 27 December 1939. To him, working for the villages was his 'life's work'. On thinking about it all, it may be relevant to understand that very little was thought or known in India, about the prevailing ideas of rural reform or rural reconstruction when the Sriniketan work was started. The goals of 'rural reconstruction', as was the terminology of the time, were to revitalize the peasantry, rebuild small enterprises, spread cooperative values, move towards localization. In Europe and the USA, those ideas were a counterpoise to the spread of industrialization and rapid urbanization. As for Rabindranath, he had begun to work in that direction from his direct experience of living close at hand to the declining villages; firstly, in his family's estates, as we already know from the earlier chapters, and subsequently, at Santiniketan, where his school was surrounded by several declining villages.

Rabindranath's response about doing something to alleviate the miseries of village life was very intimate and very direct. It was not intended to be anything revolutionary, but something that could be taken up for thought and action despite the many obstacles. Here is what he himself wrote about the Sriniketan work:

> If I were to give the details of our work they would look small. But we are not afraid of this appearance of smallness, for we have confidence in life. We know that if as a seed it represents the truth that is in us, it will overcome opposition and conquer space and time.
>
> According to us the poverty problem is not so important. It is the problem of unhappiness that is the great problem. The search for wealth which is the synonym for the production and collection of things can make use of men ruthlessly, can crush [the] life of the earth and for a time can flourish. Happiness may not compete with wealth in its list of needed materials, but it is final, it is creative, therefore it has its own source of riches within itself.
>
> Our object is to try to flood the choked bed of village life with streams of happiness.[111]

It would not be an exaggeration to say that Rabindranath had to encounter all of those things, that is, to 'overcome opposition' and to 'conquer space and time', in no uncertain measure. In short, he had to drive hard to do anything good for a better village life. As a first step, he insisted that Indians should unite to provide nation-building services to the village and not look to the State for doing what was our own duty towards our people.[112] For him, this had to be the more important function of the Swaraj being sought from alien rule.

In Rabindranath's view, what had misled society in our transition to modernity was the introduction of the Western concepts of private property and material progress. What this led to was that mankind, though never free from greed, now crossed the limits, within which it was useful rather than harmful.[113] What came about as a result was that property became individualistic and led to the abandoning of hospitality to our people and loss of communication with them. As a consequence, there was an increasing divide between city and village.[114] He found all that to be the reality, when trying to bring about changes, both in his family's agricultural estates and in the villages surrounding Santiniketan-Sriniketan.

Nevertheless, he was committed to rural reconstruction as his 'life's work' and indeed it occupied 50 years of his life, from the 1890s when he was a responsible and engaged landlord on the Tagore family estates in East Bengal, to the next four decades at Santiniketan and the surrounding villages. We read above what he wrote to Elmhirst. He wrote the same to Lord Irwin, the Viceroy, in a letter dated 28 February 1930, when appealing for a government grant towards agricultural research. 'I hope I shall have the opportunity on my return for another talk with Your Excellency in regard to *what has been my life's work* and in which I feel you take genuine personal interest.'[115] Lord Irwin had come on a visit to Sriniketan at the time and Rabindranath was told of his favourable impression of what he saw during his visit to Sriniketan. In his letter, Rabindranath wrote how he was doing the work 'almost in isolation', without any understanding from his people or from the government.

The few in his society who listened with an open mind to Rabindranath's beacon call may have understood that he was working not just to reform the villages, but also to draw the alienated Indian middle class back to its moorings. When he appealed to the educated and the young adults in his milieu, he asked them point blank to turn away from the newspapers and from politics. He asked them, instead, to come over to those with whom nobody had ever spoken, to bring them happiness and hope, to assure them that there was dignity in them as human beings, that they were not *chhotolok*. Rabindranath was desperate to shake up the deepening rift between the educated middle class and the rural populace. That was therefore an important goal in his scheme of rural reconstruction. He wrote:

> Take each of you charge of one village and organise it. Educate the villages and initiate new programmes of production and agriculture in the villages. Put new heart into the people so that they can build for themselves clean, healthy, and beautiful homes. Teach them the value of cooperative action so that they may put forward their united strength and meet their social obligations.[116]

Sadly, his love was not requited. He was held in awe and respect, but perhaps not loved and not taken to heart. He was not even given the trust he deserved. The villagers' minds were rather distracted with questions like: Have they come to exploit us? To interfere with us? To dominate us? To win piety at our cost? We know from the earlier chapters that they were suspicious even of the village work taking place in front of their eyes. They were steeped in the existing class differences. Who can tell if their suspicions might have been dowsed, if they had known that Rabindranath gave his Nobel Prize money to the Patisar

Krishi Bank to be invested in rural credit for the tenant farmers in his family estate. He refused to invest the money as an 'asset' for his Visva-Bharati University, which is what many in the Visva-Bharati University Council had expected of him. He made it clear to the University Council that the Visva-Bharati University would be entitled only to the 'interest accrued' on the Nobel Prize money paid from time to time from the Patisar Krishi Bank. The Visva-Bharati Council was not also given the authority to interfere with the investment in any way. A scholar working on this subject wrote as follows:

> Rabindranath Tagore identified the importance of rural credit as the backbone of agriculture and stressed the significance of 'krishi' (agricultural) banks. The Patisar Krishi Bank was set up in 1906 and Tagore borrowed money from his relatives and friends for the corpus fund. However, the Patisar Krishi Bank was not, as is often erroneously assumed, a 'cooperative' bank. Tagore intended it as a zamindari bank with Rathindranath Tagore [his son] as its sole proprietor.[117]

When Tagore received the Nobel Prize money, he decided to invest a large sum in the Patisar Krishi Bank in 1914. This enabled the agricultural bank to loan money to the peasants at an interest of 12 per cent per annum: a very low rate, especially in comparison to what the peasants were earlier forced to pay to the *mahajan*. Clearly, the Patisar Krishi Bank played a crucial role in releasing the peasants from the stranglehold of the moneylenders.

But the villagers' mentality was hard to crack. Just as they had no faith in themselves, they had no trust in others and no hope in anything good ever happening to them. Still, the early Sriniketan workers were so committed to their task that they stuck to their pursuit, even when repeatedly frustrated in their attempts to persuade the villagers to do what was intended for their good. We know, for example, how persistently Elmhirst himself tried to find acceptance for Sriniketan's work through the village children and the younger generation of the villages, because he found that the older villagers were unsympathetic or simply uninterested. A great deal of value was given to creating trust between 'them' and 'us'. Here is how he felt about Kalimohan Ghose and wrote:

> There was no superiority in Kalimohan. This is where Kalimohan Ghose was so valuable to us, from the outset in 1922. The villagers seemed to trust him from the moment he arrived in their village. He so enjoyed them and they certainly enjoyed him. How quickly the villagers spot whether or not you have a genuine respect and feeling for them.[118]

Despite the unavoidable disappointments, the Sriniketan programme had carried out a great deal of work for improvements in rural life. The results obtained from the various tasks were sometimes 'positive', sometimes 'negative'. Errors were assessed and discussed, as well as the achievements and failures. Elmhirst explained how he used the Charles Darwin (1809–1882) model of recording all the things that represented 'difference', by referring to the results as 'positive' or 'negative', not as 'success' or 'failure'.[119] Elmhirst frankly admitted that there were many negative results when the Sriniketan work was started. Those were faced squarely by the team. They learned from them. They chose not to run away from the negative results, but rather to work further to tackle the specific problems.

The reasons for the negative results were understandable. The Sriniketan scheme had very little funding and very few trained staff. Their working methods were flexible rather than rigorously set up and professionally taught. But the flexibility sometimes caused difficulty over staff relations. Here is an example. Somebody appointed to 'coordinate' the activities of Sriniketan found himself appointed as the Education Superintendent. That meant he had to take charge of all things, but without the authority required for an overall 'coordinator'. He could not, therefore, obtain the desired results except by his powers of persuasion among the people responsible for the different activities.

A sobering thought here is for us to try and understand that Rabindranath had very likely conceptualized an institution where there were no clear directions, no specific targets, no compulsory reports, and no red tape. Both at the top and at the bottom, much depended on the individual, the individual's commitment to the cause, and what the individual made of their job on their own initiative. Rabindranath often spoke about his faith in individuals, rather than in systems.

However, not all individuals could give their best in a free-flowing work environment. There was sometimes difficulty over interactions. At times, it was the all-too-familiar scenario of colleagues failing to get along with each other. That trend seems to have grown with the growth of the institute. By 1931, Sriniketan was already a growing institution that was living with a 10-year-old 'history' behind it, which was also a 'history' of interpersonal relationships. There were some who were drawn to its foundational ideals, while some others were not particularly so. There were some, who liked one another personally, and some, who did not. Some of them were a class apart in qualifications and skills. The better qualified were sometimes better paid. There was, for example, Hashim Amir Ali, a Cornell-trained economist, who was writing to Elmhirst on 20 July 1932 about his salary:

> When I came I found that my salary put me in a class by myself and almost alienated me from my colleagues. Gurudev in his generosity told me over and over again that I would be given full freedom, but circumstances soon taught me that however sincere the intentions, my freedom was to be a pretty anomalous freedom.[120]

There was also the vexatious and inevitable perception within the team that some colleagues had the 'ears' of Rabindranath, so to speak, whereas others did not. Elmhirst had a sixth sense about this likely problem from the beginning. He wrote for instance,

> Early on, only a day or two after my arrival in November, I had realised that Tagore sometimes made snap judgements on first acquaintance, that his enthusiasm quickly aroused could as quickly evaporate, and that until others in whom he had confidence, members of his family or staff, had reported back to him of what was afoot, he could be deeply sceptical. Knowing too of his great impatience to get the work started at Surul, I had deliberately kept away unless invited or summoned by note to discuss some specific problem. From chance remarks by Kalimohan or Santosh Majumdar, both trusted by and intimate with him [Tagore], I had realised that from the very first moment, he was immensely curious about how we were setting down to work at Surul, and that they both had had to keep him informed in detail of every move.[121]

Rabindranath was also aware about the undercurrent over staff matters and their grievances. He too had his characteristic thoughts about the vexed topic and wrote about it to Elmhirst. Astonishingly, he drew a comparison from a completely different 'setting'. It was a 'practical' observation from his experience of the river Padma, on which he often sailed, while working and living in his family's estate, from which he drew a parallel about human relationships. He wrote:

> I have seen in the river Padma, how an insignificant obstruction of a little twig or a broken pot in its bed [can help to] raise an island of sandbank in the middle of its stream within a fortnight, diverting the force of its current against a bank which had been steadfast in its service for a century. Some ridiculously small obstruction in our personal relationship, some invisible spot of irritation in our subconscious mind, is very often enough to create a vast continent of misunderstanding. Such things are daily happening in the building of all institutions, and our Santiniketan or Surul is no exception. Reports come to you not merely about the work in Sriniketan, but also about the persons belonging to it. But they are human documents and not impersonal records that science receives from nature's own archives.[122]

The problems discussed in this concluding chapter can help us to draw a few tentative conclusions with reference to the earlier chapters about the work done through the Sriniketan experiments. It should make every sense to say that the Sriniketan 'pioneers' had to deal with the most difficult and the most intricate situations, such that would have discouraged many an economist and sociologist and philosopher. The reason for this was that Sriniketan did not have any substantial support from either a government or the people it served in the villages. There was also the unmistakable truth that even within two miles of distance, Santiniketan and Sriniketan were worlds apart as institutions and as communities. Even now they are quite obviously two different worlds.

Should then one conclude that Sriniketan might have done better if it made over its task of rural reconstruction wholly to scientific experimentation? The obstacle there would have been to convince our own middle class people of the value of pure experimental work, to persuade them to accept what Elmhirst wrote, we know from above, that even a 'negative' result was as useful as the 'positive' one. Nobody, of course, could have a precise answer to what might have been the ideal approach for Sriniketan's scheme of rural reconstruction. Intuitively, one wonders if the fine balance would be to understand that while we could not fight against nature, nor overcome the social and economic factors that suppressed manhood in our country from down the centuries, we could also not leave the work entirely to getting things done from purely theoretical assumptions.

To do justice to Sriniketan we must acknowledge that their programme was seriously committed to mapping and measuring and to the other statistical parameters by following the state of knowledge of the times. We know for example that surveys were carried out and field statistics were collected and analyzed. It may not have been sustained for longer periods of study. But it is good to bear in mind when coming to our conclusions that Rabindranath's ideal of rural reconstruction was not for obtaining statistical results. He deeply believed it was not enough simply to know if the villager spun a pound of yarn or a half pound more than what he used to spin earlier or that he got from the land a maund and a half of paddy, where he used to get only one maund. He insisted that he wanted much more than that. He wanted a complete awakening of the villager's mind, so that the lowly villager could deal with the class difference into which he was born, and by which he was severely handicapped. His hope was that the villagers could still participate in the human relationship that Sriniketan's work idealized.

Rabindranath knew and consistently pointed out, as we know from the earlier chapters of this study, that Rabindranath was acutely conscious of the small scale of his work, but not apologetic for it. He said so in so many words over and over again. He reminded us that his objective was to establish an ideal, which might appeal to the country. His hope was that some of the basic principles and methods evolved through the Sriniketan experiment could be used as tools and methods for the benefit of the country in the course of time. Only one thing was urgent in his thinking and that was the need to make a beginning with the work, and not to wait. This beginning would have to have a material side of development, but it also had to have the non-material social and cultural aspects of comprehending the village and learning about it.

The sociologist, Sugata Dasgupta, who did his research directly on the Sriniketan experiment after the first few years of the pioneering period, takes us to the evolution of those ideas in the 1930s and their application over the next two decades. His research on Sriniketan was carried out in the late 1950s and published in 1962 with the title *A Poet and A Plan.* His research was carried out when some of the grassroots level workers were still participating and the work was still active. As historians, we do not have that advantage for our research. I would like to therefore depend on some of his findings, as I try to reach some conclusions on the burning question in most people's minds, even now, as to whether Sriniketan was 'successful' or not.

In this fact-finding, let me go to the end of *A Poet and A Plan* where the author provides some hard data in the form of sociological charts and also shares real life stories about some of the results. He writes:

The present author made a brief survey of the physical results of development in a few villages where the work has been conducted in a regular and systematic manner by a highly efficient Village Worker. In the village of Laldaha located thirteen miles from Sriniketan, there has thus been, by the sheer effort of the people, a thousand per cent rise in the per capita income of the people. There is 1.1 employment available for each individual in the village. No infant mortality has taken place in the area in the course of the last 6 years, and the consumption pattern of its residents has been substantially augmented.

A comparative survey of the living conditions of this village carried out in 1959 [by him] with the baseline data of 1939, recorded and maintained by the worker of the area, revealed that the people today use more clothes, furniture, utensils, torches and other equipments than they did 20 years ago and in comparison to other villages which either lay outside the work area of Sriniketan or were manned by less competent workers.

The percentage of literacy for both men and women had shot up here to 100%; 100% of the children of the school going age attended school. The recreational needs of the village were mostly met by the inhabitants themselves. The number of adults taking active interest in the development work of the area increased in the last few decades. In the cluster of villages, presented by hamlets of the Sriniketan villages of Benuria, Islampur, Bahadurpur, the percentage of literacy, both among men and women is 80%; income per capita is Rs 35, as compared to Rs 16 of the neighbouring villages.[123]

I shall use another illustration from Sugata Dasgupta's research findings, where he wrote:

> The villagers of Laldaha, when Sriniketan started its work in the year 1930, were steeped in debt and lay shackled in the hands of the indigenous money lenders who controlled their social and political destinies as well. But today the village maintains a well-organized cooperative credit society and a recent survey revealed that the people of the area owned the same volume of debts, despite the rise in prices, which they possessed in 1937. The total debt however have now contracted not from any outsiders or village money lenders but from their own cooperative organization. The credit in other words have become self-financing and productive. Not a single dispute in the village of Laldaha has been referred in the last ten years to any court of law for its settlement, all cases of conflict having been taken care of by the secular village council itself.
>
> The incidents cited here provide interesting examples of the type of development which has taken place in certain areas of the unit of operation and are drawn from the recent experiences of the present day workers. The true stories quoted above have neither been selected from a few best villages of the area only, but incidents like these, are almost daily taking place almost all over the development area of the Institute. It will however be difficult to maintain that a uniform pace of growth, material and non-material culture, has been secured in every of the area [sic].[124]

We can at least tentatively conclude that success or no success, materially or non-materially, the work was directly related to building up the power of the communities to decide on their goals and to reach their goals. Nothing was done over the heads of the communities, because the objective was *atmashakti*. Even though the success stories were patchy, it was important to keep guiding the work and expecting the communities to take it up for themselves. Better that than to keep it stagnant.

Anyone who stops to read or think about Rabindranath Tagore's mission could not fail to miss the fact that he was looking for the 'awakening' of the villager's mind. Awakening was probably the most difficult thing to attain or obtain, whatever the circumstances. That was why starting a new and alternative education was so important even with all the obstacles in the way. Nothing at all could be done till the boys and girls were 'awakened' from an early age to learn to change attitudes. Rabindranath wrote, 'Any teaching concerning man must have human nature for its chief element. How far it will harmonize with human nature is a matter of time.'[125]

Notes

Introduction

1. Christine Marsh, *Tagore Speaks to the Twenty First Century* (Devon, UK: Tagorean World, 2016), p. xx.
2. 'Abhibhasan', address to the Visva-Bharati Sammilani, 1922, in *Palli Prakriti* (Calcutta: Visva-Bharati, 1962), p. 121. Translation mine.
3. Rathindranath Tagore, *On The Edges of Time* (Calcutta: Visva-Bharati, 1958), pp. 152–3. Rathindranath was addressed as Rathi Babu in the Santiniketan-Sriniketan community. We shall use 'Rathi Babu' or Rathi for Rathindranath's name.
4. We will find Rabindranath's references to the Sriniketan work as his 'life's work' in his letters, e.g., Rabindranath to Lord Irwin, The Viceroy, 28 February 1930, English Letters', File: 'Lord Irwin', Rabindra-Bhavana Archives, Visva-Bharati University, Santiniketan; also, Rabindranath to Elmhirst, 27 December 1937, in The Dartington Hall Trust Archive, Papers of L.K. Elmhirst, LKE India, 'Visva-Bharati correspondence'.
5. *Visva-Bharati* (Santiniketan: 1929), unpaginated pamphlet.
6. Uma Das Gupta, *Santiniketan and Sriniketan A Historical Introduction*, (Santiniketan: Visva-Bharati Quarterly Booklet, 1977), pp. 30–31. [Hereafter, *Santiniketan and Sriniketan.*]
7. Partha Mitter, 'Rabindranath Tagore, Okakura Tenshin, and the creation of a Regional Modernist Art in Asia' (unpublished paper presented at the conference titled 'Concrete Media' in the Academy of Fine Arts, Vienna, 2011).
8. Partha Mitter, 'Rabindranath Tagore and the Bauhaus: A Meeting of Minds,' in *A Mediated Magic: The Indian Presence in Modernism 1880-1930*, eds. Naman P. Ahuja and Louise Belfrage (Stockholm and

Mumbai: Axel and Margaret Ax: Son Johnson Foundation and Marg Foundation, 2019), pp. 166–179.

9. Ratan Parimoo, *The Paintings of the Three Tagores* (Baroda: Maharaja Sayajirao University of Baroda, 1973), p. 118.
10. *Silpa-Bhavana, Rural Industries Department of Visva-Bharati* (Santiniketan: Bulletin no. 31, 1947), p. 5.
11. 'Path o Patheyo' (Ways and Means), 1908, essay, in *Rabindra Rachanabali*, Collected Works of Rabindranath Tagore (Calcutta: Visva-Bharati edition, vol. x, 1971), pp. 453, 458, 465–7. Translation mine.

Why Selidaha? Why Sriniketan? Why Rural Reconstruction?

12. Rabindranath to Nirmal Kumari Mahalanobis, 28 September 1930, in the Bengali journal *Desh*, Calcutta, July 1961, pp. 785–788. Translation mine.
13. *Glimpses of Bengal: Selected Letters by Rabindranath Tagore* (London: Papermac edition, 1991), pp. 25–26. Translation by Krishna Dutta and Andrew Robinson.
14. 'Sriniketan er Itihas o Adorsho', address to the workers of the Institute of Rural Reconstruction, Sriniketan, on Rabindranath's last visit there in 1939, in *Palli Prakriti* (Calcutta: Visva-Bharati Publishing Department, 1962), pp. 96–104. English translation by Marjorie Sykes titled 'The History and Ideals of Sriniketan', in *The Modern Review*, November 1941, Volume 70, Number 5, p. 5.
15. *The Religion of Man* (London: George Allen and Unwin, 1931), pp. 94–96.
16. *Rabindranath Tagore Selected Poems*, Oxford Tagore Translations, ed., Sukanta Chaudhuri (Delhi: Oxford University Press, 2004), p. 96. The original Bengali poem, 'Ebar Phirao Morey', was first published in the journal *Sadhana* (Calcutta: Chaitra 1300 / March–April 1894). Translation by Sukanta Chaudhuri.
17. 'City and Village', address delivered on seventh anniversary of the Sriniketan Institute, 6 February 1928, in *Towards Universal Man* (Bombay: Asia Publishing House, Reprint, 1967), p. 304. [Hereafter, *Towards Universal Man*.]
18. Ibid., p. 306.

19. Ibid., p. 308.
20. 'Palli Seva' (Serving the Village), essay, in *Palli Prakriti,* op.cit., pp. 65, 69. Translation mine.
21. 'Sofolotar Sodupay' (Honest Way to Our Goal), essay, in *Rabindra Rachanabali* (Collected Works of Rabindranath Tagore) (Calcutta: Visva-Bharati edition, Volume 3, 1975), pp. 570–1. Translation mine.

The Sriniketan Work Begins

22. Rabindranath to Elmhirst, 31 March 1922, in L.K. Elmhirst, *Poet and Plowman* (Calcutta: Visva-Bharati Publishing Department, 1975), pp. 18–19. [Hereafter, *Poet and Plowman.*]
23. Nripendra Chandra Bhattacharya, *John Cheap of Surul* (Santiniketan: *The Visva-Bharati Quarterly*, Volume 21, Number 3, 1955–56), pp. 1–2.
24. Ibid., p. 6.
25. L.K. Elmhirst, 'The Foundation of Sriniketan', in *Rabindranath Tagore Pioneer in Education, Essays and Exchanges between Rabindranath Tagore and L.K. Elmhirst* (Calcutta and London: Visva-Bharati Publishing Department and John Murray, 1961), p.20. [Hereafter, *Pioneer in Education.*]
26. L.K. Elmhirst's Diary, 2 July 1922, in Amar Ghosh Collection of Private Papers, Sriniketan. Amar Ghosh worked at the Sriniketan Institute from 1922 to 1956. Also, Elmhirst to Rabindranath, 31 March 1922, in 'English Letters', File: 'L.K. Elmhirst', Rabindra-Bhavana Archives, Visva-Bharati University, Santiniketan.
27. Director's Report by L.K. Elmhirst, 1922–23, in 'Sriniketan Papers', Rabindra-Bhavana Archives, Visva-Bharati University, Santiniketan.
28. Inscription in *Pioneer in Education*, op.cit., cover page.
29. Minutes of the 6th Official Meeting of the Surul Samiti, Santiniketan, 19 February 1923, Minute Book, Surul Agricultural Department, July 1922–April 1923, in 'Sriniketan Papers', Rabindra-Bhavana Archives, Visva-Bharati University, Santiniketan.
30. Sugata Dasgupta, *A Poet and A Plan, Tagore's Experiments in Rural Reconstruction* (Calcutta: Thacker Spink and Co., 1962), p. xiii. [Hereafter, *A Poet and A Plan.*]

31. 'Cooperation', essay, in *Towards Universal Man*, op.cit., p. 336.
32. 'Lokaheet', 1914, People's Welfare, essay, in *Kalantar* (Beyond the Age), (Calcutta: Visva-Bharati Publishing Department, Reprint, 1987), pp. 37–49; 'Sikshar Bikiron',1933, (The Spread of Education), essay, in *Siksha* (Education) (Calcutta: Visva-Bharati Publishing Department, Reprint, 1973), pp. 214–23.
33. Rabindranath to Elmhirst, 18 December 1928, in The Dartington Hall Trust Archive, Papers of L.K. Elmhirst, LKE India, 'Visva-Bharati correspondence'.

The Land Problem, Nationalists, and Rabindranath

34. Rabindranath to Pratima Tagore (1930), in *Letters from Russia* (Calcutta: Visva-Bharati Publishing Department, 1960), pp. 156–157. Translation mine.
35. Rabindranath to Ramendrasundar Tribedi, 20 Agrahayan 1312/ c. November 1906, in the Bengali journal *Bangabani*, Falgun 1322/ c. February–March 1916. Translation mine.
36. Rabindranath to Rathi, 7 April 1910, in 'Bengali Letters', File: 'Rathindranath Tagore', Rabindra-Bhavana Archives, Visva-Bharati University, Santiniketan. Translation mine. The phrase 'constructive swadeshi' was first used by the historian Sumit Sarkar in his book *The Swadeshi Movement in Bengal 1903–1908* (New Delhi: People's Publishing House, 1973).
37. Presidential Address, Bengal Provincial Conference, Pabna, 1908, in *Towards Universal Man*, op.cit., p. 114.
38. Binay Bhushan Chaudhuri, 'Agrarian Movements in Bengal and Bihar, 1919-39' in *Socialism in India*, ed. B.R. Nanda (Delhi: Vikas Publications, 1972), pp. 193–94.
39. Pramatha Chaudhuri, *Ryot er Katha* (About the Peasant) (Calcutta: Visva-Bharati Publishing Department, 1945), pp. 1–13. Translation mine.
40. L.S.S. O'Malley, *Bengal District Gazetteers–Rajshahi* (Calcutta: The Government Press, 1916), pp. 7–8.

The Mentality of the Villages

41. 'History and Ideals of Sriniketan', in *The Modern Review*, Volume 70, Number 5, op.cit., p.3.
42. Ibid., p.5.
43. Ibid., p.6.
44. *Letters from Russia*, op.cit., p. 117.
45. Director's Report, 1922–23, in 'Sriniketan Papers', Rabindra-Bhavana Archives, Visva-Bharati University, Santiniketan.
46. Sudhir Sen, *Rabindranath Tagore on Rural Reconstruction* (Calcutta: Visva-Bharati Publishing Department, 1943), p.170. [Hereafter, *Rural Reconstruction*.]
47. Rabindranath to Atul Sen, in *Rural Reconstruction*, op.cit., p. 164. Source of the letter is not given in the citation. Atul Sen was a worker of the Kaligram Tagore Estate. Translation mine.
48. 'Cooperation', address, in *Towards Universal Man*, op.cit., p. 336.
49. *Glimpses from Bengal*, op.cit., pp. 84–85.

Aims, Objects, and Activities of the Sriniketan Institute of Rural Reconstruction

50. L.K. Elmhirst in Foreword to *A Poet and A Plan*, op.cit., p.x.
51. *Sriniketan Institute of Rural Reconstruction*, Visva-Bharati Bulletin Number 11 (Santiniketan: 1928), p. 2ff.
52. *Siksha-Satra: An Experiment in Rural Education at Sriniketan*, Visva-Bharati Bulletin Number 21 (Santiniketan: 1941).
53. Project Number 6, Projects Book, in 'Sriniketan Papers', Rabindra-Bhavana Archives, Visva-Bharati, Santiniketan.
54. L.K. Elmhirst, 'The Foundation of Sriniketan', in *Pioneer in Education*, op.cit., p. 43.
55. Rabindranath to Elmhirst, 13 November 1922, in The Dartington Hall Trust Archive, Papers of L.K. Elmhirst, LKE India, 'Visva-Bharati correspondence'.
56. Elmhirst to Rabindranath, 28 June 1923, in 'English Letters', File: 'L.K. Elmhirst', Rabindra-Bhavana Archives, Visva-Bharati University, Santiniketan.

Agriculture and Industries at Sriniketan

57. Introduction to 'The Robbery of the Soil', lecture by L.K. Elmhirst, Calcutta, 28 July 1922, in *The Modern Review*, Volume 32, Number 4 (Calcutta: October 1922), pp.437–438.
58. *Poet and Plowman, op.cit.*, p. 146.
59. Prem Chand Lal, *Reconstruction and Education in Rural India, In the Light of the Programme Carried out at Sriniketan the Instiitute of Rural Reconstruction* (New York: Routledge Revivals, 2018), p. 63. [Hereafter, *Reconstruction and Education.*]
60. *Rural Reconstruction,* op.cit., p. xiv.
61. *Reconstruction and Education*, op.cit., p. 124.
62. Project Number 6, Projects Book, p. 50, in 'Sriniketan Papers', Rabindra-Bhavana Archives, Visva-Bharati, Santiniketan.
63. *Reconstruction and Education*, op.cit., pp. 70–71.
64. *Rural Recontsruction*, op.cit., p. 23.
65. Rabindranath to Rathi [undated, c. 1911–12], in *Chitthi Patra*, (Letters), vol. II (Calcutta: Visva-Bharati Publishing Department, 2012), in *Rural Recontsruction*, op.cit., pp. 162–163. Translation by Sudhir Sen.

The Village Welfare Department, Sriniketan

66. 'City and Village', address delivered at the seventh anniversary of the Institute of Rural Reconstruction in February 1928, in *Visva-Bharati Bulletin* (Santiniketan: December, 1928).
67. *Poet and Plowman*, op. cit., p. 155.
68. Minute Book, Volume 1, 1922–24, in 'Sriniketan Papers', Rabindra-Bhavana Archives, Visva-Bharati University, Santiniketan.
69. 'A Scheme for Cooperative Health Societies in the Area around Sriniketan', undated, in 'Sriniketan Papers', Rabindra-Bhavana Archives, Visva-Bharati University, Santiniketan.
70. 'Maternity and Child Welfare Activities', 1924, in 'Sriniketan Papers', Rabindra-Bhavana Archives, Visva-Bharati University, Santiniketan.
71. 'Quarterly Report of the Village Welfare Department', April to June

1927, in 'Sriniketan Papers', Rabindra-Bhavana Archives, Visva-Bharati University, Santiniketan.

72. *Santiniketan and Sriniketan*, op.cit., pp. 368–70.
73. *Reconstruction and Education*, op. cit., p. 89.
74. Dhirananda Ray to Elmhirst, 15 Jan 1936, in The Dartington Hall Trust Archive, Papers of L.K. Elmhirst, LKE India, 'Visva-Bharati correspondence'.
75. Rathi Babu to Elmhirst, 1 May 1927, in The Dartington Hall Trust Archive, Papers of L.K. Elmhirst, LKE India, 'Visva-Bharati correspondence'.
76. *Samaj* (Society), essays (Calcutta: Visva-Bharati Publishing Department, 1926), pp. 18–19. Translation mine.
77. *A Poet and A Plan*, op.cit., p. 102.
78. 'Sambhasan', address to the members of the 'Rabibasar' Literary Club, Santiniketan, on 30 Falgun 1343/February 1936, in *Palli Prakriti*, op.cit., p. 169. Translation mine.

Siksha-Satra and Other Educational Institutions

79. Rabindranath to Elmhirst, 19 December 1937, in The Dartington Hall Trust Archive, Papers of L.K. Elmhirst, LKE India, 'Visva-Bharati correspondence'.
80. Dhirendra Mohan Sen to Elmhirst, 1 March 1931, in The Dartington Hall Trust Archive, Papers of L.K. Elmhirst, LKE India, 'Visva-Bharati correspondence'.
81. Sriniketan Institute's 'Minute Book', Volume 1, pp. 49, 53, 'Sriniketan Papers', Rabindra-Bhavana Archives, Visva-Bharati University, Santiniketan.
82. L.K.Elmhirst, 'Siksha-Satra', in *Pioneer in Education,* op.cit., pp. 69–70.
83. Section on 'Old Students' in *Siksha-Satra: An Experiment in Rural Education at Sriniketan,* op.cit., pp. 12–13.
84. *Silpa-Bhavana: Rural Industries Department of the Visva-Bharati,* Visva-Bharati Bulletin Number 31 (Santiniketan: 1947), p. 6.
85. List of Lantern Lectures for Village Training Camps, in 'Sriniketan Papers',

Rabindra-Bhavana Archive, Visva-Bharati University, Santiniketan.

86. Kalimohan Ghose, *SriniketanPalli-Seva Vibhag er Pratibedan*, Published Report of the Sriniketan Department of Village Welfare Department (Santiniketan: 1924), pp. 3–4.

87. Uma Das Gupta, 'A Bibliographical Note on the Sources of Sriniketan History, 1922–1941' in *Visva-Bharati Journal of Research, Humanities and Social Sciences,* Volume 4, Part 1, 1979–80 (Santiniketan: 1980), pp. 82–84.

88. Ibid., pp. 85–86.

Anti-Malaria Research and Cooperative Health Societies

89 L.K. Elmhirst, 'The Foundation of Sriniketan', in *Pioneer in Education,* op.cit., pp. 38–39.

90. 'Information on the First Five Cooperative Health Societies under Sriniketan', in 'Sriniketan Papers', Rabindra-Bhavana Archives, Visva-Bharati, Santiniketan.

91. *A Poet and A Plan*, op.cit., p. 60.

92. Tribute to Dr Harry Timbres by C.F. Andrews, in the *Visva-Bharati Annual Report*, 1937 (Santiniketan: 1937).

93. *Health Cooperatives*, Visva-Bharati Bulletin no. 25 (Santiniketan: 1946).

94. Ibid.

95. This information was obtained from my interviews with Hemanta Sarkar on 14 April and 7 May 1978. Hemanta Sarkar was sent by the Sriniketan Institute as a Village Worker to stay at Ballavpur from 1928 to 1931 to guide them in the application of the Sriniketan programme. Later he took charge of Sriniketan's Weaving Department from 1931–35. Subsequently, he resigned from the Sriniketan Institute.

96. *Rural Survey: Ballavpur* (Sriniketan: 1940). See Appendix.

97. Information obtained from the 'Papers of the Ballavpur Samiti for 1929–30' in the Private Collection of Sridhar Bhattacharya, then resident of Ballavpur.

Sriniketan in the 1930s: A Changing Scenario

98. Lord Sinha to Elmhirst, 26 October 1926, in The Dartington Hall Trust Archive, Papers of L.K. Elmhirst, LKE India, 'Visva-Bharati correspondence'.
99. Lord Sinha to Elmhirst, 3 February 1927, in The Dartington Hall Trust Archive, Papers of L.K. Elmhirst, LKE India, 'Visva-Bharati correspondence'.
100. Rathi Babu's Reorganisation Scheme for Sriniketan, 1934, in 'Sriniketan Papers', Rabindra-Bhavana Archives, Visva-Bharati University, Santiniketan.
101. Sriniketan Institute's Minute Book, Volume 2 (1932–36), pp. 448–49, 'Sriniketan Papers', Rabindra-Bhavana Archives, Visva-Bharati University, Santiniketan.
102. Project Nos. 1, 2, and 3, 'Sriniketan Papers', Rabindra-Bhavana Archives, Visva-Bharati University, Santiniketan.
103. This information was obtained from my interviews with Hemanta Sarkar at Sriniketan on 14 April and 7 May 1978.
104. *Silpa-Bhavana, Rural Industries Department of the Visva-Bharati,* Visva-Bharati Bulletin Number 31 (Santiniketan: 1947), p. 8; and *Development of Cottage Industries by Silpa-Bhavana*, Visva-Bharati Bulletin no. 32 (Santiniketan: 1951), p. 4.
105. Ibid., p. 6.
106. Rathi Babu to Elmhirst, 12 August 1940, in The Dartington Hall Trust Archive, Papers of L.K. Elmhirst, LKE India, 'Visva-Bharati correspondence'.
107. *Silpa-Bhavana,* op.cit., p. 7.
108. Ibid., pp. 8–11.
109. Rathi Babu to Elmhirst, 7 November 1938, in The Dartington Hall Trust Archive, Papers of L.K. Elmhirst, LKE India, 'Visva-Bharati correspondence'.

Some Endemic Problems, Some Tentative Conclusions

110. Rabindranath to Elmhirst, 27 December 1939, in The Dartington Hall Trust Archive, Papers of L.K. Elmhirst, LKE India,

'Visva-Bharati correspondence'.

111. 'Introduction' to L.K. Elmhirst's lecture titled 'The Robbery of the Soil', Calcutta, 28 July 1922, in Sisir Kumar Das ed., *The English Writings of Rabindranath Tagore*, Volume 3 (New Delhi: Sahitya Akademi, 1996), p. 871.
112. 'Swadeshi Samaj', essay, in *Swadeshi Samaj* (Calcutta: Visva-Bharati Publishing Department, 1962), pp. 21–22, 23–25. Translation mine.
113. 'Bilaser Phans', (Luxury's Trap), essay, in *Samaj*, op.cit., pp. 18–19. Translation mine.
114. 'City and Village', essay, in *Towards Universal Man*, op.cit., p. 309.
115. Rabindranath to Lord Irwin, The Viceroy, 28 February 1930, in The Dartington Hall Trust Archive, Papers of L.K. Elmhirst, LKE India, 'Visva-Bharati correspondence'.
116. Presidential Address, in *Towards Universal Man*, op.cit., p. 125.
117. Swati Ganguli, 'A Poet and a Landlord: Rabindranath Tagore and the Nobel Prize money', in *Economic and Political Weekly*, Mumbai, Volume 49, Number 3, August 2014, pp. 140–41.
118. Discussion between Rabindranath and Elmhirst cited in the Foreword of *A Poet and A Plan*, op.cit., p. ix. In this Foreword Elmhirst referred to his 'old notebook' as the source from which he recalled the discussion.
119. Ibid., pp. x–xi.
120. Hashim Amir Ali to Elmhirst, 20 July 1932, in The Dartington Hall Trust Archive, Papers of L.K. Elmhirst, LKE India, 'Visva-Bharati correspondence'.
121. *Poet and Plowman*, op.cit., p. 121.
122. Rabindranath to Elmhirst, 21 October 1926, in The Dartington Hall Trust Archive, Papers of L.K. Elmhirst, LKE India, 'Visva-Bharati correspondence'.
123. *A Poet and A Plan*, op.cit., pp. 112–13.
124. Ibid., pp. 123–24.
125. Rabindranath to Elmhirst, 3 September 1932, in The Dartington Hall Trust Archive, Papers of L.K. Elmhirst, LKE India, 'Visva-Bharati correspondence'.

Bibliography

Archival Sources

'Sriniketan Papers', Rabindra-Bhavana Archives, Visva-Bharati University, Santiniketan

'Bengali Letters', File: Rathindranath Tagore, Rabindra-Bhavana Archives, Visva-Bharati University, Santiniketan.

'English Letters', File: L.K. Elmhirst, Rabindra-Bhavana Archives, Visva-Bharati University, Santiniketan.

The Dartington Hall Trust Archive, Papers of L.K. Elmhirst, LKE India, 'Visva-Bharati correspondence'.

Printed Archival Sources

Visva-Bharati Bulletins (in chronological order)

Prospectus of Apprenticeship and Training Camp, Institute of Rural Reconstruction, Sriniketan, Visva-Bharati Bulletin no. 6 (Santiniketan: 1928)

City and Village, Visva-Bharati Bulletin no. 10 (Santiniketan: 1928)

Sriniketan Institute of Rural Reconstruction, Visva-Bharati Bulletin no. 11 (Santiniketan: 1928)

Siksha-Satra: An Experiment in Rural Education at Sriniketan, Visva-Bharati Bulletin no. 21 (Santiniketan: 1936)

Health Cooperatives, Visva-Bharati Bulletin no. 25 (Santiniketan: 1938)

Loka-Siksha Samsad, in Bengali, Visva-Bharati Bulletin no. 26 (Santiniketan: 1940)

Silpa-Bhavana, Rural Industries Department of Visva-Bharati, Visva-Bharati Bulletin no. 31 (Santiniketan: 1947)

Development of Cottage Industries by Silpa-Bhavana, Visva-Bharati Bulletin no. 31 (Santiniketan: 1951)

Rural Surveys and Statistical Enquiries

Kalimohan Ghose, *Rural Survey Ballavpur*, Visva-Bharati (Sriniketan, 1926)

Kalimohan Ghose, *Rural Survey Raipur*, Visva-Bharati (Sriniketan, 1933)

Rural Survey Supur, Visva-Bharati (Sriniketan, 1933)

Hashim Amir Ali, *Three Village Economic Studies on Rice*, Visva-Bharati Rural Studies, 1, 2, 3 (Sriniketan, 1934)

Harry Timbres, *Records of the Malaria Survey in Villages in West Bengal* (1935)

Fliers and Information Sheets

Why You Should Support the Work of Sriniketan

Summary of Health Work Activities

Catalogue of Sriniketan Handicrafts

Sriniketan and the New Education Fellowship: A Conference of Primary School Teachers, 1936

Prochar Patromala (Fliers in Bengali)

'Palli Samaj er Gorar Kotha'

'Krishi Unnati'

'Nobanna Utsav'

'Malariar Protikar'

'Santal Kendrey Palli Sangathon'

Select Writings by Tagore

Tagore, Rabindranath, *Chitthi Patra*, (Letters), vol. II (Calcutta: Visva-Bharati Publishing Department, 2012)

__________________, *Glimpses of Bengal Select Letters 1885-1895* (New Delhi, Niyogi Books, 2018)

__________________, 'History and Ideals of Sriniketan', *The Modern Review*, (Calcutta, November 1941, vol. no.

__________________, *Kalantar* (Beyond the Age) (Calcutta: Visva-Bharati Publishing Department, Reprint, 1987)

__________________, *Letters from Russia* (Calcutta: Visva-Bharati Publishing Department, 1960)

__________________, *Palli Prakriti* (Calcutta: Visva-Bharati, 1962)

__________________, *Samaj*, (Calcutta: Visva-Bharati Publishing Department, 1926)

__________________, *Swadeshi Samaj* (Calcutta: Visva-Bharati Publishing Department, 1962)

__________________, *Siksha* (Calcutta: Visva-Bharati Publishing Department, Reprint, 1973)

__________________, *The Cooperative Principle* (Calcutta: Visva-Bharati Publishing Department, 1963)

__________________, *The Religion of Man, Being the Hibbert Lectures for 1930* (London: George Allen and Unwin, 1931)

Select Writings by Others

Chaudhuri, Pramatha, *Ryot er Katha* (Calcutta: Visva-Bharati Publishing Department, 1945).

Chaudhuri, Sukanta ed., *Rabindranath Tagore Selected Poems*, Oxford Tagore Translations (Delhi: Oxford University Press, 2004).

Das, Sisir Kumar, ed., *The English Writings of Rabindranath Tagore*, vol. 3, (New Delhi: Sahitya Akademi, 1996).

Dasgupta, Sugata, *A Poet and A Plan, Tagore's Experiments in Rural Reconstruction* (Calcutta: Thacker Spink and Co., 1962).

Das Gupta, Uma, *Santiniketan and Sriniketan: A Historical Introduction*, (Santiniketan: Visva-Bharati Quarterly Booklet, 1977).

Das Gupta, Uma, *Rabindranath Tagore: A Biography* (Delhi: Oxford University Press, 2004).

Das Gupta, Uma, ed., *Rabindranath Tagore: My Life in My Words* (Delhi: Penguin Books, 2006 and 2010).

Dutta Krishna and Robinson, Andrew, eds., *Glimpses of Bengal: Selected Letters by Rabindranath Tagore* (London: Papermac edition, 1991)

Elmhirst, L.K., *Poet and Plowman* (Calcutta: Visva-Bharati Publishing Department, 1975).

Lal, P.C., *Reconstruction and Education in Rural India, In the Light of the Programme Carried out at Sriniketan the Instiitute of Rural Reconstruction* (New York: Routledge Revivals, 2018).

Marsh, Christine, *Tagore Speaks to the Twenty First Century* (Devon, UK: Tagorean World, 2016).

O'Malley, L.S.S., *Bengal District Gazetteers–Rajshahi* (Calcutta: The Government Press, 1916).

Parimoo, Ratan, *The Paintings of the Three Tagores* (Baroda: Maharaja Sayajirao University of Baroda, 1973).

Rabindranath Tagore Pioneer in Education, Essays and Exchanges between Rabindranath Tagore and L.K. Elmhirst (Calcutta and London: Visva-Bharati Publishing Department and John Murray, 1961).

Sen, Sudhir, *Rabindranath Tagore on Rural Reconstruction* (Calcutta: Visva-Bharati Publishing Department, 1943).

Sinha, Dikshit, *Rabindranath er Pallypunargathan Prayas*, in Bengali (Kolkata: Paschim Banga Bangla Akademi, 2010).

Sinha, Dikshit, *A Poet's Experiment in Rebuilding Samaj and Nation* (Bolpur: Birutjatiyo Sahitya Sammiloni, 2019).

Tagore, Rathindranath, *On The Edges of Time* (Calcutta: Visva-Bharati Publishing Department, 1958).

Articles and Conference Papers

Bhattacharya, Nripendra. 'John Cheap of Surul.' *The Visva-Bharati Quarterly* (1955–56) 21 (Winter): 3.

Chatterjee, Sukumar. 'The Cooperative Health Societies Under the Visva-Bharati.' *The Modern Review* (1940) 67 (May): 5.

Chaudhuri, Benoy Bhusan. 'Agrarian Movements in Bengal and Bihar, 1919–39.' ed. B.R. Nanda. *Socialism in India* (1972).

Das Gupta, Uma. 'Rabindranath Tagore on Rural Reconstruction: The Sriniketan Programme, 1921–41.' *The Indian Historical Review* (1978) IV: 2.

Das Gupta, Uma. 'Sriniketan 1921–41: A Bibliographical Introduction', *Visva-Bharati Journal of Research* (1979–80) 4: 1.

Das Gupta, Uma. 'Santiniketan and Sriniketan', *Introduction to Tagore, Visva-Bharati Text Book on Tagore Studies* (1983).

Elmhirst, L.K. 'Sriniketan.' *The Visva-Bharati Quarterly* (1995) 21 (September): 2.

Mitter, Partha. 'Rabindranath Tagore, Okakura Tenshin, and the creation of a Regional Modernist Art in Asia.' Unpublished paper presented at the conference titled 'Concrete Media', Academy of Fine Arts, Vienna (2011).

Mitter, Partha. 'Rabindranath Tagore and the Bauhaus: A Meeting of Minds.' eds. Naman P. Ahuja and Louise Belfrage. *A Mediated Magic: The Indian Presence in Modernism 1880–1930* (2019).

Sen, Sudhir. 'Conflict of Economic Ideologies in India: An Attempt at Reconciliation.' *Visva-Bharati Economic Studies* (1940) 1.

Appendix I

Rural Survey
Ballabhpur

RURAL SURVEY

BALLABHPUR

SRINIKETAN

Edited by Kalimohan Ghosh

Village Welfare Department.

Visva-bharati] [Price 6 annas.

PREFACE

There is no difference of opinion as to the fact that the urban ways of life have attacked the very heart of rural society, and are daily bringing about vital changes therein. We have now to find out methods by which our decaying villages can be brought back to life. For this, some villages of different districts of Bengal should first be thoroughly surveyed and facts should be carefully collected relating to their economic and social condition.

Since the very foundation of Sriniketan our revered Founder President, Rabindranath Tagore has been insisting on our taking up rural survey work, and asking us to collect necessary materials. We had not been able to begin this important work ourselves for want of time and proper experience, so now we appointed Prof. Rajanikanta Das, M. A. Ph. D. to guide us in modern methods of Village Analysis and Regional Survey.

We had, however, not gone far when Dr. Das was compelled by unavoidable circumstances to go back to Europe. We now depended on the practical training we had received from Dr. Das to guide us in our work, and encouraged by Srijut Rathindranath Tagore we proceeded in our investigations. This book embodies fully the facts we collected about a single village named "Ballabhpur".

For the pictures in this booklet we have to thank Silpacharyya Srijut Nandalal Bose, and his two pupils Sjts. Masoji. and Hariharan.

Sj. Hemantakumar Sarkar, a new and enthusiastic worker of the Village Welfare Section, Sriniketan, has laboured tirelessly for the cause. Sjts. Dhirananda Roy, and Sasadhar Mukherji, have also rendered us valuable service. To all of them we offer our grateful thanks.

Generally the villagers do not like to answer any questions regarding their own village, they feel suspicious. This attitude of theirs create difficulties which are apt to appear insurmountable ; and it is no small credit to our workers that they have been able to win their way through, such resistance and made possible an intensive study of village conditions. It is our sincere hope that we shall be able to carry out our scheme of rural survey work more systematically and with greater accuracy in the light of further experience.

VILLAGE WELFARE DEPARTMENT.
Sriniketan, Ashar, 1333. (July 1926).

Kalimohan Ghosh
Secretary

The Village of Ballabhpur

Ballabhpur is a village in District Birbhum, 4 miles distant from the town of Bolpur. The Kopai river flows along its Western and Northern boundaries. This river is dry in the hot weather, but becomes a torrent during the rains, flooding the low lying land to its north, which therefore is the most fertile portion. The Western and Southern portions are high land sloping towards the river, and consequently not admitting of being irrigated from the river. The soil of this high land is of a stony hardness in the dry weather, but is easily softened during the rains. It is composed of a reddish soil, mixed with coarse sand, pebbles and calcareous nodules. To the South of the village there is a large excoriated tract of land full of rubble through which the rain water flows into the river. This is called the *khoai* and is over a mile in length, portions of it extending upto the village of Surul. At one time this tract was covered with a forest of Sal trees, being then called **Ban Ballabhpur,** (Ballabhpur forest or wood) and the roots of the trees then protected the surface from denudation. Indiscriminate destruction of this forest for firewood seems to have led to its present ravine-like condition.

The average annual rainfall in Bolpur during the last 15 or 16 years has been 54. 14 inches. The climate is dry and usually healthy. The direction of the wind is mainly from the South East in the hot weather and from the North West in the cold weather.

The area of Ballabhpur is 3744 biggahs comprised as under:

Jungle & Khoai	–2748. 36 biggahs.
Homestead	42
Tanks	42
Fallow grazing grounds	201
Other land	710. 64
	3744

Population—The total number of inhabitants (in 1332 B. S.) is 84. They numbered 100 in 1327. During these five years 4 families have become extinct. Others have left the village, living at present only 24 families. These comprise the following castes,

Higher—

Brahmin	...	6 families.	Comprising 38 members Average 3. 2 per family.
Weavers	...	3 „	
Potter	...	1 „	
Barber	...	1 „	
Tamli	...	1 „	

Lower—

Cobbler	...	7 „	Comprising 46 members Average 3. 8 per family.
Hadi	...	2 „	
Dom	...	3 „	

The women outnumber the men by 9. Boys : 14. Girls : 10.

Previous History

In the days of the East India Company Mr. Cheap came here as Commercial President and set up his place of business to the South of Ballabhpur near the North West corner of Surul. In his time there were 500 families living in the village. Cheap used to export textile fabrics and manufacture sugar. He had also Indigo plantations in the District. It was owing to the employment available in connexion with Mr. Cheap's concern that this forest village came to attain such large dimensions. Cheap died in 1824 A. D. and thereupon with the cessation of the business the village began to decay.

Livelihood

Of the present population of 84 all except 7 who are labourers depend on Agriculture for their living.

The weaver family consists of 4 members. They have one loom which turns out only 4 yards of *gamchas* (flimsy country towels) per month. They keep up the loom more as a caste tradition, but rely mainly on cultivation. The potter family, however, earn their living mainly from their caste occupation.

Trees

The valuable trees in the village are :

Mango	...	30
Bel-fruit	...	18
Guava	...	3
Date	...	618
Palmyra	...	700
Tamarind	...	6
Vabula	...	1
Bamboo Clumps		68

Besides these there are some Palasa trees on the border of the *khoai*. At the South end of the village the Zemindars have a large house and garden. This being practically outside the village and of no concern to the villagers, its trees have not been included in the above enumeration.

Birds—Owing to the scarcity of fruits and grain Birds are few. Crows, kites, *mynas* and paddy-birds are to be seen. There are also partridges.

Classification of Land

The land is locally classified as follows :—

Do land—This is land suitable for winter rice. It can also bear pulses, til-seed, sugar-cane, and cotton. It is subdivided into first, second and third class.

The first class Do land yields good autumn rice. The rice crop is reaped in the month of Aswin (August—September) and thereupon the land is manured and ploughed for pulses or mustard. Potatoes also grow well on this class of land. These crops ripen in the winter, whereupon *Til* is sown, and by the time this ripens the time for sowing rice comes round again.

The second class Do land requires more irrigation and yields less. On this onions and garlic grow better than pulses or mustard. The third class Do requires still more irrigation and yields still less.

Suna land—This retains moisture well and requires irrigation largely, so that it is not suitable for sugar cane. It is more expensive to cultivate. It yields less of *rabi* crops.

Sali land—On this the winter rice is grown. When the rice crop ripens, the *khesari* pulse is sown in between. The soil is a moist clay.

Olan (low) land—This receives the river silt after the rains, and is consequently very fertile. But the floods damage the crops. Melons and certain vegetables are chiefly grown.

Danga (high) land. Arhar, Son-hemp and brinjals are grown.

Pat or Tut land. (a) **Dihi tut**—High land near the homesteads suitable for mulberries.

(b) **Mathal Tut**—High land away from the village. Not so good as the **Dihi tut.**

Jungle land—Sal trees flourish on this.

Ghas land—grows a variety of fodder grass. After the first crop is cut, it is left fallow for pasture.

Reeds—Grow plentifully on the river side. They are used for thatching being laid under the straw as they are not attacked by white-ants. Also used for making shaded greenhouses for growing the betel vine.

Vastu land (homestead)—(a) homestead proper.

(b) Outlying compound round homestead. The latter is of two kinds,—within the fencing where vegetables are grown and outside the fencing for fruit trees. These last usually lie fallow owing to the depredations of baboons.

Sal ghar—These are the spaces on which the sugar-cane is pressed.

Fallow land—is of four kinds

(a) **Sabek patit or danga patit**—(originally fallow). This is rent-free.

(b) **Hal patit** or **fasal patit**—This lies fallow because of irrigation difficulties and is cultivated in years of heavy rainfall.

(c) **Rasad patit**—land of doubtful ownership allowed to be retained by the nearest tenant rent-free so as to protect it against adverse possession.

(d) **Gochar patit**—(grazing commons). All the villagers are allowed to graze their cattle on this free of charge.

The soil is locally classified according to quality as follows :—

Metel mati (a damp clayey soil) suitable for rice, sugarcane, wheat, gram and pulses.

Etel mati—(a stiff clay) this is yellowish in colour very sticky when moist, and very hard when dry. Suitable for rice only, not rabi crops.

Bagha etel—(variegated in colour) contains lime, can grow rice if well manured, but nothing else.

Pali mati—(silt receiving). Yellowish in colour, loose, very fertile, suitable, in addition to all the other usual crops, for potatoes and vegetables. Not used for rice, as being less valuable. Does not usually require irrigation ; suitable for pottery work.

Bindi mati—A sandy loam, reddish in colour, cannot retain moisture.

A dark variety of this has more clay in it and is suitable for all kinds of crops including rabi if irrigated.

There is also a light-coloured variety with more sand, which cannot grow rabi crops.

Where the rubble is in excess only coarse crops can be grown such as millet and cow-pea.

Land under cultivation—is 457 biggahs. About 100 biggahs more are suitable for cultivation, but are not cultivated owing to irrigation or money difficulties. Of the cultivated land 4 biggahs are Etel (clay). 4 biggahs *kakor* (rubbly) and 449 biggahs sandy loam. 4 biggahs on the river side yield 2 crops annually ; 2 biggahs are under sugercane. On 2 biggahs potatoes are grown after the rice crop is reaped, the rest of the cultivated land is under rice only.

Tenancies—155 biggahs are retained by the Zemindar himself, 302 biggahs are farmed out to tenants, 236 biggahs to resident villagers, and 66 to outsiders. Nine families sublet their tenancies to cultivators on the half-and-half system. Seven families employ servants to plough for them. Eight families consisting of 30 members hold no land.

Most of the tenancies are permanent, but are all held under occupancy tenure

Rent—is from Re. 1/12 to Rs 2/—per biggah payable in 3 kists per year in money.

The total collection from this village is Rs 900 a year. There are no other exactions. Interest is charged on default at 2 annas in the rupee. There has been no enhancement of rent during the last twenty years.

Cultivation

Yield of crops :—The average annual yield is :

Paddy 5 mds. per big.
Potatoes 25 mds per big.
Molasses 20 " "

The soil has not improved but rather deteriorated in fertility during the last 5 years.

Noxious Insects.—A black caterpillar (called Pangapoka) attacks the rice plants cutting away the stem near the root, in years of excessive rainfall, when the field remains long under water.

Bullock Cart

A picture is given above of the type of bullock carts used here. The names of the different parts of the cart are given below.

1. (১) *Odal* (back portion)
2. (২) *Chaka* (wheal)
3. (৩) *Mige* (axle)
4. (৪) *Jown* (yoke)
5. (৫) *Sholi* (hook)
6. (৬) *Eguri* (front-part—Driver's seat)

Granary

Paddy for use for a whole year is generally kept in a granary by the cultivators and householders. These granaries are made with straw twisted into ropes; the top is thatched with straw. The thatch is removed in order to draw the grains out from within. Unlike the common ones, there is no door to this type of granary. A picture of it is given below :

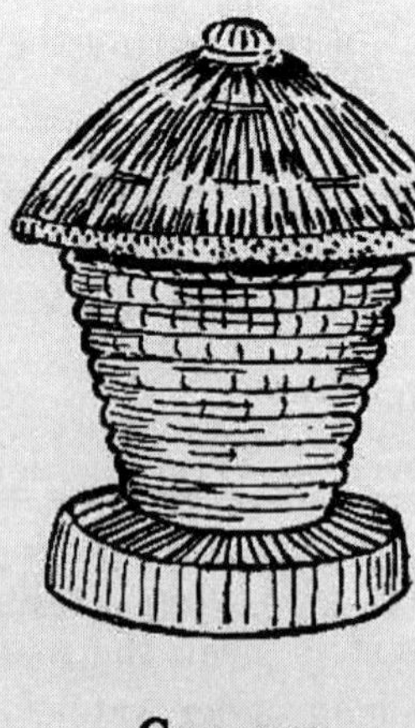

Granary

A kind of blight (majra) attacks the sugar cane if the rain holds off too long.

The cultivators do not know of any remedy for these.

Manure.—This differs with the kind of crop.

For rice--2 carts of cowdung per biggah.

For potatoes 10 " " "

For Sugarcane 15 " " "

Besides cowdung, silt from tanks, ashes and oilcakes are also used.

From the month of *Baisakh* manure is distributed on the ground. It is carried in a *Khatla* (large basket) on a cart. This *Khatla* is made with straw done into ropes and then woven together. A picture of a *Khatla* is given below.

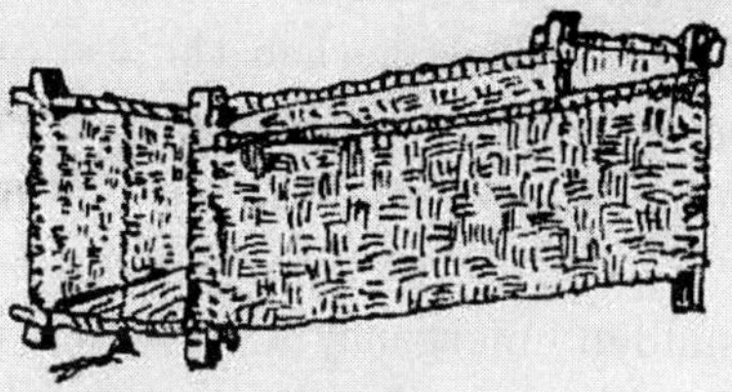

Khatla.

Labour.—To prepare the ground one cultivator takes

for rice - 3 days per biggah.

for potatoes - 6 " "

Rice

Three varieties of rice are usually grown :—

1. **Aus** or Early rice of two kinds, red and white.

2. **Katke** or late rice (ripening in Kartik) (October-November) of 4 kinds *Nayankalma, Sadai sal, Kashiphul* and *Nabine* or *bak chuda.* This is so-called because is harvested in the month of Kartik.

3. **Bara-dhan** or winter rice (bigger kind). These are of many varieties, such as, Sindurmukhi, Jatakalma, Kalikalma, Bachaikalma, Kanakchud, Hanyakhudi, Barakalma, Hatishal, Bansgajal, Lalnona Dhakinona, Latamul, Latasal, etc. These are mostly coarse.

Rice-seed is stored in a dry separate room in earthen or tin vessels.

The cultivators exchange their surplus seeds with one another so that each one may have a chance of growing different varieties.

The paddy (about 50 maunds a year) is sold to the merchants or rice mills in Bolpur where it is taken in carts. The price this year is Rs. 4-8-0 per maund.

Ploughing

13 to 15 biggahs can be ploughed with one plough and a pair of bullocks at the rate of 25 kottas per day. Ploughs are not hired.

The Gata System—There is a system of co-operative ploughing called *gata*, which is as follows :—

(1) If one cultivator assists in the ploughing of a neighbour's field he can claim in return from the latter a like amount of labour for his own field.

(2) If the latter (the original recipient of help) has no plough and bullocks, he must give three days' labour without plough in lieu of one day's labour with plough. If he had the use of plough and bullocks only then he would have to give in return 2 days' labour only.

(3) Similar exchanges would apply to digging reaping threshing etc.

(4) If on a sudden emergency a cultivator requires extra men he invites his neighbours who render him willing assistance with labour and implements, in which case all they expect by way of return is a feast.

Sugarcane cultivation—The system of co-operation in this case is a survival of age-long system. Sugar cane is deemed to be a product of the first importance and its cultivation is the ambition of all cultivators. The cultivation of sugarcane with hired labour, however, entails an expenditure of Rs 152 per bigha and yields a profit of Rs 47,—which is not deemed adequate for the outlay. Hence this is but rarely undertaken. The successive operations of cutting the cane, taking it over to the pressing place (where shelter against rain is erected), taking over the cane to the press, dressing the cane by taking off the leaves, putting the cane into the press, driving the bullocks working the press, and boiling the juice and making the molasses are all comprised under the term *shal*. The *shal* system of co-operation is as follows :—

A leader is first elected who will direct the operations. The leader hires the press on his own responsibility, either at a daily rate or on a contract for the season, the latter being the cheapest. The season is for 3 months from Magh (January—February) to Chaitra (March—April) and the hire for such season is from Rs 30 to Rs 35. A further economy can be effected in case their own work is completed before the expiry of the term, by subletting the press to others, sometimes at a rate sufficient to cover the whole or greater part of the hire. This is accordingly the more usual form. The daily rate is from Re. 1/- to Rs 1/4. This is availed of by those who have a comparatively small crop to deal with and are not in a position to sublet the press.

The press being hired, the leader calls upon each cultivator to supply men or bullocks in proportion to his crop. These men foregather at the appointed time and place. Their first duty is to erect the shelter mentioned before. Then in accordance with the directions of the leader the cane is cut and brought in from the different fields in turn, and subjected to the series of operations detailed above. Work goes on day and night in shifts arranged by the leader until the entire crop of the village has been dealt with. The juice extracted after 24 hours of work absorbs the produce of about 5 kottas of land and amounts to 15 maunds. It takes 6 men and 6 pairs of bullocks to keep a press working for 24 hours. Besides these it takes 4 men to feed the press and boil the juice so produced. The boiling pan holds about 35 seers of juice. One man with one pair of bullocks has to work till one pan is full. This takes from 1 to 1½ hours according to the strength of the bullocks. 6 men relieve one another in turn, the first coming back after the sixth, each man and pair of bullocks thus working thrice during the 24 hours and producing 3 pans of juice. An attempt is made so to arrange the shifts that each cultivator may have to labour in proportion to the quantity of his crop. This however does not always work out accurately in practice. The leader has to furnish his quota of bullocks, but is exempt from labour, which he gets free for his crop.

Cotton—50 or 60 years ago cotton used to be grown in this village, but there is no remnant of it now.

Irrigation—Some 8 to 10 biggahs on the river side can be irrigated from the river.

There are four tanks for irrigation in the village, but as they dry up by Chaitra (March-April) in each year (being replenished during the rains) they are capable of irrigating only 4 to 5 biggahs in their present condition. While the water level of the tank is high, the water is drawn through channels cut for the purpose. When the water level is low the water has to be lifted by a kind of trough. If these tanks were cleared of silt and deepened they could irrigate at least 60 biggahs. In order to get all the land irrigated four more big tanks would have to be excavated. Two of the tanks are owned by or under the control of the Zemindar but he takes no trouble about improving them. Another is owned by 7 muchis and the third by 2 Brahmins—all too poor to attempt any improvements.

In other parts of the district attempts at improving tanks have been made by forming Co-operative Irrigation Societies. The difficulty in this village is that though many of these cutivators requiring irrigation are willing to co-operate, a certain number of them are incorrigibly factious and obstruct all such endeavours. By damming the *khoai* and filling it with water from the river, a large reservoir could be formed but this would be an expensive undertaking.

The owners of the tanks do not cut the channels, but leave that to be done by the cultivators requiring the water, with the result that they cannot agree among themselves and often fail to get the work done in time.

Bullocks -of these there are 36. There are no Buffaloes.

Krishans—(labouring cultivators) are those who work on others' fields ; the ploughs, bullocks and other necessaries being supplied by the owner. They receive a share of the produce, but not of the straw. Where the owner of the land only supplies manure and seed, and the *krishan* has to provide his own plough and bullocks, he gets a half share of the produce.

Income from Rice Cultivation

The cost of rice-cultivation per biggah is as follows :

3 days' labour for ploughing etc. @—/8/—per day	Rs.	1—8—0
Food for one pair of bullocks (24 bundles of straw per day)		1—0—0
$1\frac{1}{2}$ seers oilcakes		0—1—6
Seed 5 seers		0—6—0
2 hands for sowing		1—0—0
4 hands for hoeing		2—0—0
1 hand for reaping ($1\frac{1}{2}$ days)		0—12—0
3 hands for threshing		1—8—0
Cowdung 2 carts		1—8—0
Cartage to carry to market		0—4—0
Total	Rs.	9—15—6

The yield per biggah is 5 mds. of paddy @ Rs. 4/—average—	Rs.	20/—
Straw	...	9/—
Total	Rs.	29/—

Thus a profit of Rs. 19—0—6 is left.

Income from Potatoes

The cost is as follows :

6 days' labour for preparing ground @ —/8/—	...	Rs. 3—0—0
Bullock feed (24 bundles of straw per day)	...	2—0 0
(3 seers oil cake)	...	0—3—0
Cowdung 10 carts @ —/12/— ...	...	Rs. 7—8—0
Oilcakes 2 maunds ...	...	5—0—0
Seed 2½ mds ...	...	25—0—0
12 hands for sowing @ —/8/— ...	...	6—0—0
9 hands for irrigating (3 times) ...	...	4—8—0
16 hands for digging, making furrows etc.	...	8—0—0
8 hands for digging out potatoes ...	...	4—0—0
Cartage to market ...	...	2—0—0
	Total	Rs. 67—3—0

The yield is 40 mds per biggah @ 2/8 ... Rs. 100/—
leaving a profit of Rs. 32/13/—

Income from Sugarcane

The cost is as follows :

8 days' labour for preparing ground @ —/8/—	...	Rs. 4—0—0
20 carts cowdung		
5 mds oil cake ...	...	27—8—0
Food for Bullocks. Straw & Oil cake ...	...	3—0—0
Seed 5 measures ..	...	25—0—0
10 hands for planting out seed ...	...	5—0—0
Irrigation (10 times during 9 months) 20 hands	...	10—0—0
Attending to crop while growing ...	...	40 0—0
Stands for cutting the cane ...	...	2—8—0
10 hands from preparing cane for press ...	...	5—0—0
Hire of Press ...	..	5—0—0
10 Bullocks (4 days' food) ...	...	7—8—0
Pressing and boiling ...	...	12—0—0
Cost of receptacles ...	..	5—0—0
Cartage ...	...	1—0—0
	Total	Rs. 152—8—0

The yield is 20 mds. of molasses per biggah @ 10/— ... Rs. 200/—
leaving a profit of Rs. 47—8—0.

The results under the co-operative system above described are better.

Domestic Animals

These number 207 valued as under :

Bulls 2 @ 15/	...	Rs	30/—
Bullocks—36 @ 35/	...		1260/—
Milk cows 77 @ 16/	...		1232/—
Calves 50 @ 4/—	...		200/—
Goats 40 @ 4/—	...		160/—
Pigs 2 @ 8/—	...		16/ -
	Total	Rs	2, 898/ –

Cattle—Of the 77 cows 14 or 15 give milk, the rest are dry. The daily yield is 8 seers per day for the whole village. The price of pure milk is 6 seers to the Rupee. The fallow lands are used for grazing,—about 200 biggahs.

Fodder—Consists of grass and straw with an addition of oil cakes for the plough-bullocks. Not more two thirds of the quantity required is obtainable locally, the straw being primarily used for thatching and only the surplus as fodder, which suffices only for 5 months' feed in the year.

The local straw is not exported. The price is Rs. 18/- per kahan of 1280 bundles. 3 years ago the price was Rs. 7 per kahan. Grass is available on the grazing grounds for 3 months in the year but as outside cows are also allowed to graze, the village cows do not get the full benefit even of this. The food thus sufficing for 8 months only has to be eked out during the whole 12, with the result that the cows are half-starved and are getting thinner and weaker and in every way poorer.

There is a cattle market at Sukbazar 10 miles from this village.

Breeding—No trouble is taken in regard to breeding. The old practice of keeping common bulls at large is not kept up. The herdsmen (Rakhals) graze all the cows together, weak and diseased animals promiscuously with the rest.

Diseases—In the year 1331 B. S. (1924—25) 15 cows died of Rinderpest which was been raging in this locality for years, destroying thousands of cattle. The District Board has not so far been able to do anything to check the ravages of this disease.

The diseases to which the local cows are subject and their treatment are given below : –

[13]

Colic—(Wind in the stomach). One or two lice in half a pint of country spirits are administered internally.

Spleen—When a cow trembles all over and falls down with convulsive movements of the legs, it is said to have the "spleen." Some Omar bel fruit and 21 pepper seeds are macerated with the water from the hookah (saturated with tobacco products) and administered internally.

Foot disease—a sore within the cleft of the hoof in which a kind of worm is found, which makes the cow limp. The worm is extracted if possible, and the sore washed first with carbolic oil or phenyle, and then plastered with a mixture of lime and tobacco.

Damp lameness—This occurs during the rainy season. The diseased animal trembles and limps. The smoke of burning paddy husks is held to the nose. Human hair covered with lime is bound round the horns. Drinking cold water is considered to be fatal, warm rice gruel is given instead.

Rinderpest—There is no proper systen of segregation so that the disease has been raging unchecked. There is no regular veterinary physician. Two persons is the village are supposed to know something about the treatment of cows.

Cowherds—Each villager has his own cowshed. Those who have many cows engage a cowherd. The others join together to engage a common cowherd who takes the cows to the grazing ground at about 8 O'clock in the morning and brings them back at about 3 O' clock in the afternoon. The remuneration of the cowherd employed by one master consists of a pair of dhoties and a gamcha at the time of the Durga Pooja (Autumn), a vest or shirt and coarse cotton sheet as a wrap in the winter, a further pair of dhoties in the summer. This is besides his daily meals and other refreshment. They get Rs. 5 to Rs 6 in money during the year. Common cowherds charge one anna per cow as wages, and also get tips at Pooja time. If a cow calves on the grazing ground, the cowherd gets a *gamcha* as his perquisite.

Goats—are kept in the cowsheds.

Pigs—Low shelters are separately erected for these of a size sufficient for the herd.

Poultry—Fowls and ducks are kept by Haris, Doms and Mochis but not by the higher castes. There are no pigeons.

There are altogether :—

Cocks	...	8
Hens	...	17
Chickens	...	17
Drakes	...	1
Ducks	...	1
	Total	44.

The fowls weigh from half to one seer. The hens lay from 40 to 60 eggs in the year weighing between an ounce and an ounce and a half. The hens can sit on 12 to 14 eggs at a time. The eggs are kept in a corner of the living room on sand or straw and there the hen broods, chiefly during the rainy season, which is chosen because the chicks can find green grass and suitable insects, and the crows and kites, their chief enemies leave the village to hunt for their food in the flooded fields. Eggs are thus plentiful for selling and other purposes in the summer and winter. As cocks are sufficiently numerous the eggs are mostly fertile.

The fowls are fed on rice, unhusked, husked or boiled, the chickens on rice powder, in addition to the insects etc they can pick up for themselves.

Buying and selling—The villagers get their requirements from the Bolpur market. All crops are also sold in Bolpur.

There is no co-operative buying or selling. There are no middlemen.

Communications—The District Board road from Suri to Burdwan passes by this village, and a 4 mile feeder road from Bolpur joins it at Surul. No co-operative schemes exist with regard to the buying and selling of these roads.

Indebtedness.

These borrow money from the Zeminder of Surul and the Bhattacharyya family of Goalpara. 75% of the village people use cloths produced by the mills in this country. There is a *gola* (granary for stocking paddy) but there is no stock of paddy in any one's house. The annual produce of paddy is used up in the same year. There is no *Dharma-gola* (or Co-operative granary). Jute, wheat, linseed and mustard are not grown in this village. Cane-sugar grinding mills are in operation here.

Fish.

No fisherman lives in this village the villagers occasionally catch fish for themselves, the *Keots* (a kind of fishermen) of the neighbouring village sometimes helping them in procuring fish. They do not export fish from the village, because of the paucity of fish there.

Cloth.

The villagers buy Rs. 860 worth of cloth annually. 75% of the villagers use cloth made by country mills, and by hand-looms, and buy *gamchas* made by the local weaving class. At the time of ploughing, the cultivators buy *gamchas* 3½ cubit in length, and these are supplied by the village *Tantis* (weavers). The local weavers use thread from the Dunbar cotton mills. Effort was once made to introduce threads produced by the Banga Luxmy mills, but the weavers did not like that because the hanks were not equal ; and this caused inconvenience to them. The people of this village annually buy foreign made cloth of the value of about Rs. 215-1-0 Every family needs on the average cloth of the value of Rs. 35-13-6 pies.

About one-twentyfourths of the grain is exported from the village. This village does not produce any vegetable, the people buying them from the *hat* (periodical market).

Family budget.

A Brahmin family has five dependents, among them two are adult men, two adult women, two minor girls. A statement of the income and expenditure of this family was taken in the Bengali year 1332.

This family has thirty *biggahs* of land. About seven years go five *biggahs* of land were under sand, and does not therefore. yield any crop yet. Land is generally cultivated by local cultivators.

The sources of income are seven ;—

(1) Produce of the land.
(2) Priestly profession.
(3) Rent.
(4) Salaries.
(5) Sale of milk.
(6) Sale of manure.
(7) Sale of fish (from ponds).

Income.

Total income from land		Rs. 708-8-0
Paddy—133 maunds— ..	Rs. 540 0-0	
Straw—7 *kahans*— ...	Rs. 126-0-0	
Potato—10 maunds— .	Rs. 25-0 0	
Turmeric—3 seers— ...	Rs. 1-0 0	
Flax seeds ...	Rs. 2-0-0	
Rent collection ...	Rs. 14-0-0	
	Rs. 708-8-0	
Income from the services of priests and preceptors		Rs. 244-4-0
Dakshina (fee of the priest) ...	Rs. 179-3-3	
Pranami (present to the priest) ...	Rs. 29-12-0	
Tailabat (honorarium for religious direction from the priest) ...	Rs. 8 11 6	
Parbani (festive gifts) ...	Rs. 2-0-0	
Sale of rice received as gift ...	Rs. 2-9-9	
Cloth received as gifts ...	Rs. 20 13 0	
Rent of *Debottar* land ...	Rs. 1-2-0	
	Rs. 244 4 0	
Wages		Rs. 107 3-0
Income from cows		Rs. 71-4 0
$4\frac{1}{2}$ maunds milk produced in the house at the rate of 6 seers per rupee	Rs. 30 0-0	
Cowdung as manure, 55 cartloards	Rs 41-4 0	
	Rs. 71-4-0	
Fish from pond—15 seers		Rs. 7-0-0
Grand Total		Rs. 1138-3-0

Expense

Annual food Expense Rs. 376-3 9

Rice—24 maunds	...	Rs. 168-0 0
Flour	...	Rs. 8 2 0
Pulse	..	Rs. 11-9 6
Vegetables	...	Rs. 41-7 9
Fish	...	Rs. 13 14 6
Oil	...	Rs. 18-10 0
Salt	...	Rs. 3-5-0
Spices	...	Rs. 21-2-6
Milk	...	Rs. 39 1-3
Ghee	...	Rs. 2-0 0
Sugar, treacle and Sweets	...	Rs. 9-9 3
Fuels (wood and coal)	...	Rs. 12 9-9
Kerosine	...	Rs. 8-4-9
Cocoanut oil	...	Rs. 2-8-9
Betel-leaves, nut and lime	...	Rs. 3-12-9
Soap, Soda	...	Rs. 1-8 6
Tobacco	...	Rs. 7-10-9
Liquor, hemp, hemp-leaves	...	Rs. 2-14-9
		Rs. 376-3-9

Yearly expenditure on clothes Rs. 49-11-9

Sari 4 pairs	...	Rs. 17 0-0
Dhuti 4 pairs	...	Rs 14 0-0
Gamcha 8 pieces	...	Rs. 3 0 0
Bedsheet 1	...	Rs. 1-4-0
Jacket 1	..	Rs. 1-11-9
Coat 2	..	Rs. 6-4 0
Banyan	...	Rs. 1-4-0
Shoes 1 pair	...	Rs. 5-0-0
		Rs. 49-11-9

Medical Expenses Rs, 15-8-6

Expenses for cultivations			Rs. 243-15-6
Labourers' wages for ploughing 25 biggahs of land	...	Rs. 188-13-0	
Manure	...	Rs. 49-10-0	
Seed for paddy and potato	...	Rs. 15 8 6	
		Rs. 243-15-6	
Expense for cow keeping			Rs. 153-6-9
Fodder for 5 cows, 2 bullocks, 10 calves	...	Rs. 133-14 9	
Salary for cowboy	...	Rs. 19-8-0	
		Rs. 153-6-9	
Miscellaneous family Expenses			Rs. 71-12-6
Puja Expense	...	Rs. 49 0-3	
Ceremonial gifts and offerings	...	Rs. 7-8-0	
Railway travelling	...	Rs. 21 4-0	
Debt and interest repayment	...	Rs. 35-0-6	
Revenue	...	Rs. 37-6-0	
Union Board tax	...	Rs. 1-8-0	
Subscription to Co-operative Village Union	...	Rs. 3-0-0	
			Rs. 154-10-9
Grand Total			Rs. 1065 5 6

Total income	...	Rs. 1138-3-0
Total Expenditure	...	Rs. 1065-5-6
Surplus		Rs. 72-13-6

Remarks

The net produce of paddy is in certain years, considerebly reduced in this place owing to scarcity of rain. In the Bengali years 1322—23—24 owing to continuous drought the produce of rice fell consecutivly for three years & therefore the income of this family did not reach the normal level. The head of the family borrowed Rupees 500/- at the interest of Rs. 15½% for the marriage of himself and his brother. The debt could not be cleared because of the income going down due to above reasons.

This family is comparatively affluent in the village ; like other families it enjoys the income from the land ; but it has the additional advantage, unlike others of the village, of earning an extra income through priestly profession and preceptor's work.

A poor family of the untouchable caste has three dependants including one adult man, and a minor girl.

A statistics of the income and expenditure of the family was taken in the Bengali year 1332. In that year it succeeded in earning something by taking on rent a few date palm trees and producing treacle from them. But this opportunity does not occur every year. The head of the family owns twenty five *kothas* of land, and he cultivates on share two *biggahs* of land. He does not possess his own ploughs. He cultivated the land on *hetel* principles (reciprocal labour-interchange system).

The family has four sources of income—

1. Cultivation
2. Production of *Khejur* treacle
3. Wages
4. Paddy husking

Income

Total income from cultivation		Rs. 58-0-0
Two maunds paddy from his own land ..	Rs. 8-0-0	
Paddy plus one-fifth *kahan* straw ...	Rs. 3-10-0	
Cultivation on share, 8 maunds paddy plus four-fifth *kahan* Straw (Rs.32 + Rs. 14-6-0) ...	Rs. 46-6-0	
	Rs. 58-0 0	
Price of locally produced date palm treacle	Rs. 30-0-0	
Labour ...	Rs. 2-0-0	
Price of husked paddy 6 maunds ...	Rs 36-0-0	
Total income	Rs. 126-0 0	
Annual food expense		Rs. 157-5-0
Rice $22\frac{1}{2}$ mds. ...	Rs. 135 0 0	
Pulse 6 seers ...	Rs. 1-5 0	
Vegetables and fish ...	Rs 6 0 0	
Mustard oil 9 seers ...	Rs. 6-12-0	
Cocoanut oil $2\frac{1}{4}$ seers ...	Rs. 1-11-0	
Salt 10 seers ...	Rs. 1 8-0	
Kerosine oil 9 seers ...	Rs. 2 4 0	
Tobacco 15 seers ...	Rs. 2 13-0	
	Rs. 157-5-0	

Annual expenditure on clothes		Rs. 15-14 0
Dhuti 3 pairs ...	Rs. 7-0 0	
Sari 2 pairs ...	Rs. 8-0.0	
gamcha 1 pair ...	As. 0-14-0	
	Rs. 15-14-0	
Annual expenditure on medicine		Rs. 6-0 0
Annual expenditure on cultivation		Rs. 3-10-0
Four cartloads of manure (2 for private land and 2 for land held in share ...	Rs. 3 0 0	
Paddy seeds ...	As. 0-10-0	
	Rs. 3-10-0	
Rent of land		Rs. 1-8-0
House rent		As. 0-6-0
Liquor		Rs. 3-0 0
	Total expenditure Rs.	187-11-0

Total expenditure	Rs. 187-11 0
Total income	Rs. 126-0-0
Debt	Rs. 61-11-0

The householder did not borrow the amount of Rs. 61-11-0 in cash, a person in the village gave him a loan of 15 maunds of rice, the rest, Rs. 1-11-0, was borrowed in cash. Nothing of the borrowed paddy has yet been repaid by the householder.

The paddy-crop of his own land was not satisfactory last year ; good crop was returned from two biggahs of land cultivated in share. This man has been suffering from malaria for a year, with enormously enlarged spleen and liver. He could not undertake any field-work because of his illness.

His homestead consists of only one thatched cottage. He sleeps inside and cooks in the verandah.

Last year they could not drink any milk. Even the infant daughter was not given milk for a day. They cannot prepare any tiffin of flattened rice, fried rice or puffed rice, because of poverty ; they have to take ordinary boiled rice thrice a day.

Out of 48 inhabitants of the village 33 spend their days in poverty like this or in a worse manner.

The condition of the touchable caste is mostly like this.

Loom

In the time of Mr. Cheap this village was inhabited by 60 families of prosperous weavers. The head-man of this weaving colony was the late Kailashchandra Dutta who died at the age of 100 years. He used to do various works when Mr. Cheap's factory was established. We have collected this piece of information from the daughter in-law of Kailash Babu's sister's son.

Thirty or forty years ago cloths used had no border attached to them but there were broad *anchla* (hems) of high colour. Even now Mahomedan women use *anchlas* manufactured by country-weavers. Mill-made cloths were introduced twenty five years ago. There were borders to such mill-made cloths ; the country-weavers imitated them, and attached blue borders to the cloth manufactured by them.

Thirty five years there were 15 weavers family in the village, at present there are only three families and there is one male amongst them. Formerly the weaver in the village used hand-driven shuttles, adult weavers could produce daily ten yards of cloth. The weaver who lives there works at his loom in his leisure-time and produces from 70 to 80 yards of cloth per month. Now-a-days weavers use yarns of 12·5 and 16·5 counts. The yarn traders of Bolpur import them from the Dunbar mills. Labour costs about 2 as per yard in weaving cloth with yarn of 16·5 count. Thak-Thaki (hand-driven) looms are still used in the village. Nobody spins any yarn in this village because the price of cotton is high and there is no local cotton at all, and because the income from spinning is very meagre.

The opinion of an old woman of 65 years is that at present the men and woman of a family do not want to use coarse cloth. The change in the taste of people is the cause of the disappearance of the spinning wheel.

The women belonging to other castes than the Brahmins husk rice at their leisure and the lower caste women serve as day-labourers. These working women are called *kamins.*

Other Crafts.

No shoe maker tans leather in this village. There is production of earthen-ware The village potter produces earthen-ware sufficient for the needs of the whole village, and so the potter lives fairly well. There is no festival or periodical fair or exhibition in the village.

Labour.

About ten years ago the rate of wages was 3 annas per day ; it has increased gradually, rising today to eight annas daily. The people of the village think that this increase of wage is due to the following causes.

Within the last few years twenty four rice mills have been established in Bolpur. Due to the want of coolies the mill-owners are increasing the wages competitively. Every labourer works seven hours a day. The *Hadi, Dom* and *Muchi* castes work as coolie, and farm-labourer, and cultivate land in share. When the tilling of land comes to a stop, they earn their living by labouring on wage, and they generally work in land within a distance of three or four miles from the village.

In the *Muchi* caste there is one well-to-do family which owns about twenty biggahs of land. The *Muchis* spend their time in repairing their own houses and walls, and working on their own lands. The labourers generally keep away from work on festive occasions. They have to sit idle when they cannot find any work or when they fall ill. Otherwise they do not absent themselves from work.

The time for work is from eight to twelve in the morning, and from two to five in the afternoon. As they start from home for work they take with them some *mudi* (fried rice) in a corner of their cloth, and with this they make their tiffin after twelve o'clock. On the average they are unable to get work for four or five days in the month.

For the last few years almost every wage-earner fell ill with fever during the malaria season.

Debts.

Out of 24 families 23 are in debts. They run into debts on account of *Sraddha* ceremonies and for illnesses. In this village money-lending business is led by the Zemindars of Surul, the Bhattacharyyas of Goalpara, and the *Kabulis* of Bolpur. The money-lenders of the locality charge from 12 to 30% interest on capital lent out, while the *Kabulis* exact from 150 to 175 per cent. When the local money lenders lend out capital, money does not generally accumulate on account of the mortgage of the borrower's land. The *Kabulis* lend money to the lower caste people without mortgage, but extract payment on the strength of their *lathis*. When one or two poor people stealthily leave the village because of the pressure of their debts, the *Kabulis* have to suffer loss.

Realising money by law-suits.

A total expenditure of forty rupees is necessary for stamp-fee, pleader's fee, tips to peons and clerks, charges for witnesses etc for realising a sum of rupees one hundred. Out of this expenditure rupees twenty may be paid by the debtor, the other half being sheer loss to the money lender.

All debts are generally realized in this village as the money-lenders try to get their money back during the months of *Magh* and *Phalgun*.

There is only one man in the village who is free from debts, and this man is a Muchi by caste. He has twenty biggahs of land and he is very laborious and earns wages by hard work whenever there is any opportunity.

Relatively low rate of interest is available when money is borrowed on mortgage of land, the rate being never more than 12 to 18 per cent.

Social facts

In the village of Ballabhpur there are three untouchable castes (water touched by them being unacceptable to other castes), viz the *Hadis*, the *Doms*, and the *Muchis*. The *Muchis* occupy the north of the village, the *Hadis* the south, the *Doms* the middle part. Each caste lives in a locality aloof from others. There are five classes among the touchable castes ; they are, the *Brahmins*, the *Tantis* (weavers), *Tamulis* (betel-sellers), the *Napits* (barbers) the *Kumbhakars* (potters).

There is an underlying unity in the several castes inspite of their differences. During festivals and ceremonies people of all castes gather together and enjoy the time unitedly. On the last day of the great Autum-festival known as the *Durgotsab*, the villagers meet and embrace and salute one another, feeling great joy in mutual companionship.

Besides, the Brahmins go to the houses of the touchable caste and make enquiries whenever there is illness, and persons of the touchable castes in their turn go to the houses of the *Brahmins* and help in their work as far as possible, but from outside. In physical strength the untouchables are superior to the touchables, but the higher castes are morally much better than the lower ones. The lower castes are remarkable for their frankness, neighbourly sympathy and truthfulness. Education has brought higher ideals to the upper classes, but the lower castes, because of their ignorance, are yet absolutely inert and without modern ideas. They possess no ambition and are very timid ; they are afraid of the higher castes and even of speaking out their minds. Manliness has been totally destroyed in them by social injustice.

Drink

Both men and women of the lower castes drink wine. The men frequent the fermented liquor shop on their way home from daily labour but the women drink only on festive occasions. At marriage and *Sraddha* ceremonies the young and old, men and women drink plentifully. During festive occasions they may do without rice, but they are censored by relatives and friends in case liquor is not supplied.

Marriage

The girls of lower caste are married from the age of three to thirteen, and the boys from sixteen to twenty-three. Widow-marriage is prevalent among the untouchables, as well as freedom for women. Further, the custom of divorcing the husband and taking to a "companion" (a second husband) is obtained among the untouchables.

Religion.

All the inhabitants of this village are *Hindus*. Though the local *Muchis* are equally *Hindus* yet they eat the flesh of the cow that may be left in the village dumping ground. Generally these *Muchis* consider cow-killing a heinous offence and they never do it.

The following religious festivals are observed in the village :

1. In a Brahmin's house the Durga Puja is performed in the Autumn.

2. A common Kali Puja is performed unitedly by the villagers in the month of Kartik.

3. The Dharma Puja is performed whenever there is full moon in the month of Baishakh. This is a time of great jubilation in the village, and all join in this Puja irrespective of caste.

Dharma or Dharma Thakur is the accepted village god. This god is worshipped generally in every village of this district. Goats, sheep, ducks, fowls and swine are sacrificed to this God. Formerly a piece of black stone used to be placed at the foot of a tree and worshipped; now a thatched temple has been built there.

Pastimes.

No game is prevalent in this village as the number of boys and young men is very small indeed. No sign of activity in this respect can be noticed in them because of their bad health, generally caused by malaria. The inhabitants of the village at times arrange singing parties and sing religious songs (*Kirtan*).

Pictorial Art.

There is an old and dilapitated temple in the village. A phallic symbol of Siva had been established there. Two or three women of the village can do *alpana* drawing, ie. decorations with rice paste. At marriage ceremonies *pidis* (wooden seats) are painted with *alpana*. Winnowing fans are not painted in this way. A Brahmin woman can do fine needle work, and generally, all women are used to sewing *kantha* (thin quilts made of old linen),

Culture.

In every community, high or low, there is want of honesty ; yet in this village false cases are comparatively few. The lower caste people seem to be more frank. Hospitality of the olden times is no longer found in the village, the beggars, however, are not disappointed by any body, and food is given to the hungry traveller. Mutual confidence is not available, some sort of confidence has been introduced among men here by the establishment of the Co-operative Society, and its work for the last two years. The workers of the Village Welfare Society are loved and trusted by all ; yet, at the time of collecting information we were looked upon with eyes of suspicion.

Good advice is listened to with interest, but the villagers have no great desire to turn it into action. The whole village seems to be lifeless, signs of some energy are evidenced in the meetings of the Society. Among high ideals, that of *Dharma* is trusted Through the worship of the God *Dharma* and through the singing of religious songs, the great ideal of "Kindness to all beings and faith in the name of God" is still faintly present everywhere.

The people do not enyoy good health like the *Santals*, nor are they so joyful. The spirit of unity, enthusiasm and energy found among the Mahomedans is sadly missed in the people of this village. The ancient system of the *Panchayet* is not now found in the village.

The Union Board realizes Rs. 32-12-0 as tax from this village, but the Board does not spend anything for its health and improvement. There is a *Chowkidar* in the village on a salary of Rs. 6/- a month, but he does not regularly attend to his duty of watching. Generally, quarrels are settled in the house of the local Zemindar.

The Zemindar.

Srijukta Debendránath Sarkar, a descendant of the *Sadgop* family of Surul is the Zeminder of this village. He is a lawyer practising in Burdwan. Outside the village, and on the bank of the river, the Goddess *Siddheswari* is worshipped in the month of Pous. He himself joins in the ceremony aud contributes a good sum to it. He does not oppress his tenants, but he does not take much trouble for the improvement of his village.

Only three men of the village have the right to vote for the election of a member to the Provincial Council.

Liquor-shop.

There is a liquor shop in the village for selling fermented liquor. This sort of liquor is produced by the fermentation of rice. About 12 mds. of rice is required each month for this shop. The liquor that is thus produced is priced at Rs. 16/- per maund of rice, making a total of Rs. 192/- in the month, and Rs. 2304/- in the year.

Payment of Commission to the Government	...	Rs. 575 0-0
Price of 144 mds. rice at the rate of Rs. 6/- per maund	...	Rs. 864 0-0
Other ingredients for preparing liquor	...	Rs. 30-0-0
Total expenses		Rs. 1469-0-0

Annual income of the shop Rs. 2304 – Rs. 1469 = Rs. 835-0-0

Liquor is drunk by men from tin mugs, a seer of liquor costs an anna.

Theft and Robbery

During the last five years there has been no robbery or murder in the village, but, every year small thefts take place occasionally. Last year there was only one case of theft. Paddy was stolen thrice, and once about 2 maunds of potato. There was no litigation between the inhabitants of the village within the last three years.

Roads

There was an old road in the village, both sides of which were overgrown with woods. This road fell into bad condition with the deterioration of the village. Under the auspices of the Village Council the woods on either side of the road were cut down and cleared in the Bengali year 1332. Drains have been dug on both sides of the road and the earth thus obtained has been spread on the surface of the road. There are four lanes altogether on both sides of the road, and bullock carts can be driven on only two of these lanes, while, the other two do not allow any cart due to their narrowness.

The villagers use cowdung cakes for fuel. Their need is not met by the fuel that is obtainable here.

The name of the Village

Nobody can say anything as to the history and source of the name of the village. Before the arrival of Mr. Cheap, this village was called Bana-Ballabhpur as there were thick woods in it, and this has already been referred to.

Manuscript Books

The following manuscripts are preserved in the house of Srijukta Shashibhushan Bhattacharyya—

1. The grammar of Panini
2. Hindu law and custom (Smriti)
3. The Bhagabata (Purana)
4. Dashakarma Paddhati (Rules for the ten ceremonies)

A few manuscripts were collected from this house for the library of the Visvabharati. The late Srijut Madhuṣudan Bhattacharyya, the elder brother of Mr. Bhattacharyya was a good Sanskrit scholar. He had the reputation of being a learned man, he also followed the priestly profession. He was very clean in his habits, amiable, and loved by every-one. It is his manuscripts that have been spoken of above. He lived up to the age of 97 years and died about six or seven years ago.

Health

The health of the village was very unsatisfactory about 2 years ago, but recently slow improvement is taking place in this direction through the combined efforts of the villagers. There has been no epidemic in the village during the last five years, but Malarial attacks are rather common. Out of 84 inhabitants of the present day 17 are suffering from Malaria.

22 persons have died in the village during the last five years ; comprising 10 men, 6 women, and 6 children ; all died of malaria. There was no case of sudden death during this period.

There is not a single doctor is the village ; in case of illness the villagers have to get a doctor from Sriniketan or from the town of Bolpur. The fee paid to a doctor from Bolpur in generally Rs. 4/-. For the last two years arrangements have been made for the services of an M. B. passed doctor by the Village Welfare Society at a small cost, as described below.

Self-reliance is the first step to progress. The Visvabharati Village Welfare Society has made it possible that those villagers who combine to improve the health of the village and give their time and energy to it, will have the privilege of having the qualified doctor of the Visvabharati Village Welfare Society for treating on half fee cases of illnesses in their villages, they also get medicines from the Sriniketan Dispensary at a nominal cost. The inhabitans of Ballabhpur having formed them selves into a Village Welfare Society are making use of this privilege by calling in the doctor according to need on a fee Rupee one only, and medicines at the trifling cost of one anna per bottle.

Formerly there was in the village no means for the outflow of water. The village grew unhealthy because of water accumulating in the hollows on both sides of the road and even on the surface of the road itself. Since the foundation of the Village Welfare Society a good road has been laid out through the heart of the village, and drains have been dug on both sides. This improvement of the village drainage has secured comparative improvement of the health of the inhabitants.

There is no fixed place in the village for burying dead cattle and birds, the carcasses of the cattle are generally thrown away here and there at places outside the village.

The inhabitants have no conservancy system like those of the towns.

The health of the village has gone down because of the causes mentioned above. The water of the ponds has become undrinkable on account of unhealthy practices.

The villagers generally drink the water from the neighbouring *Kopai* river. The water thereof does not dry up in the summer, but about knee-deep water is found in it even at that time. In the rainy season the water becomes turbid. The villagers then allow the water to stand in a vessel for a day and then use it for drinking purposes.

In the summer when the heat is terrific, buffaloes and cows get into the river for washing and cooling themselves and this also makes the water dirty and unfit for drinking purposes.

The houses in the village are made of mud walls and straw thatch, there is no brick-built house here. Generally the rooms are very small and windows are wanting, hence free ventilation is not avaiable. The area of rooms, generally, is 1620 cubic feet, three people live in a room of this type; therefore every person gets about 540 cubic feet of space. Some houses are surrounded by jungles, and the outskirts are unclean, there are, however, exceptions.

The villagers generally do not use mosquito curtains. Out of 24 families only 5 have such curtains. The comparatively well-to-do people use bedsteads, the rest sleep on the floor. The daily meal of the villager usally consists of rice, pulse and some vegetables. Fish is not available at all times. On the average, adults take one *Poua* of rice. During the last five years 29 babies were born in this village—9 boys, 20 girls.

Malaria.

In the year 1924 malarial patients of this village brought medicines no less than 96 times from the Sriniketan Dispensary during the malaria season, and 56 times in the following year. There is a Health Association in the village and so the villagers get medicines and the help of the doctor from Sriniketan, and never go elsewhere. We find that there is a reduction of 41% in cases of malaria in this village. In the neighbouring villages about 45% of the inhabitants had malaria last year. We can point out more directly to the results of the activities of the Welfare Society after some years more.

Village Health-Association and its work.

In order to free the villagers from malaria and other diseases the Village Welfare Society of Sriniketan, established on a co-operative basis in this village in the Bengali year 1332 an Association for village reconstruction and for the improvement of health. At present there are only 23 members, among whom are men of all castes such as Brahmins, Barbers, Potters, Shoe-makers, and others.

Rules of Association.

Everyone has to pay a monthly subscription of 4 as. in order to be a member of the Association. Out of these four annas, an anna is credited in the name of the contributor for buying a share of the Association, and the other three annas are spent for improving the health conditions of the village. Those members who are poor and are unable to pay the regular subscription are required to contribute half a day's manual labour to works relating to the health-improvement of the village. Instead of paying them in cash annas 4 for their work, their labour is considered as their contribution, and according to the rule above a share of the Association is credited in their favour.

It has alrealy been described in detail how the Village Welfare Department of Sriniketan arranged for the medical treatment of the members of this Association. In November 1925 this Association was registered according to the Rules of the Government Co-operative Department. It regularly receives aid every month from the Birbhum Dirtrict Board which contributes an amount equal to what is obtained from local subscriptions and by other means.

The following works were undertaken by the Association during the last 8 months.

1. Two stagnant pools were filled with earth.
2. A jungle was cleared from a piece of land covering $12\frac{1}{4}$ biggahs.
3. 17 date palm-trees were cut down.
4. A road was made from one end of the village to the other measuring 440 yards in length and 3 yards in breadth.
5. Narrow drains were dug on both sides of the road and through these all the water of the village flows out.
6. In order to prevent the breeding of Anophelis mosquitos all the ponds of the village were treated with kerosene oil during the malaria season.

The members of the Association were given, during the malaria season quinine worth Rs. 4-12-0 in total.

The income and expenditure of the Association for the last 8 months are given below.

Income.

Subscription from the members of the Association etc.		Rs. 46-0-0
Received from the District Board	...	Rs. 45 8-0
	Total	Rs. 91-8-0

Expenditure.

For road-making and drain-digging	...	Rs. 39-4-0
For filling up pools	...	Rs. 7-14-0
Clearing jungles	...	Rs. 22-0-0
Kerosene oil	...	Rs. 1-2-0
Quinine	...	Rs. 4-11-0
Establishment Expenses	...	Rs. 0-8-0
Miscellaneous	...	Rs. 1-2 0
	Total	Rs. 76-9-0

Income	...	Rs. 91-8 0
Expenditure	...	Rs. 76-9-0
	Balance	Rs. 14-15 0

Education

Upto the year 1314 there was a *Tol* in the house of Srjukta Sashibhushan Bhattacharyya. His elder brother the late pandit Madhu-bhushan Bhattacharyya was a teacher of the *Tol.* 7 or 8 students were kept by him in his house ; he used to supply them with food and never charged any fee from them ; only clothes were brought by them from their own homes.

But at present the condition of the education in the village is very unsatisfactory. There is not a single *Tol, Pathsala* or Night School for the education of the boys. 2 boys are reading in Surul, a village at a distance of two miles. One of them is aged 10, the other 14. Each pays a fee of annas 4 per month. The village has no library ; no newspaper is read by the villagers as they have no curiosity for outside news, due to chronic economic distress. Recently the villagers have started reading books from the village library of the Village Welfare Department of the Visvabharati. The number of literate people in the village is only 13, the remaining 71 are illiterate ; no one in the untouchable caste can read or write. For them there is no Free School, nor any technical institution.

Among educated men in the village there are—

(1) One who is trained in sanscrit and strictly observes the ten orthodox injunctions, (2) four who know how to read and write in Bengali, (3) two who can sign their names in Bengali ; (4) one who can sign his name in Urdu ; (5) one who has studied up to the first year 1 A ; (6) two women who have just a little education.

Lectures were arranged by the Village Welfare Section of Sriniketan on the following subjects—

(1) The health of the Village, (2) Social customs and traditions, (3) Character building.—There were also other lectures on related subjects. Lectures were illustrated by means of lantern slides, but only four of them were delivered last year.

The village people do not generally go to places other than the houses of their relations. Elderly people occasionally go away on pilgrimage to holy places.

Out of the nine educated people seven live in the village. Of these seven one earns his livelihood by cultivation and priestly profession, two by cultivation and service in a zemindary office, one by cultivation and weaving, one by cultivation and by his caste trade of pottery making, another by cultivation and his caste-trade as barber and a little of carpentery.

That villager who read upto the 1. A. standard lives at a distance of four miles from the village, he teaches the children of the Zemindar in the village of Taltali. He gets his food there besides Rs.12/- as monthly salary. He has an elder brother at home who follows the priestly profession and of whom mention has been made above. Another villager works in a shop at a place named Bandhgora at a distance of 2 miles. He gets his food when he works there, he owns thirty five biggahs of land and has to depend mainly on this land for his own livelihood and for the maintenance of his family.

Excepting these two, the others do not live away from the village for the the sake of earniug.

Appendices

Population

	Names	Castes	Men	Women	Girls	Boys	Total No.
1.	Sridhar Bhattacharyya	Brahmin	1	0	0	1	2
2.	Panchanan Bhattacharyya	„	1	1	1	2	5
3.	Sambhunath Mukhopadhyaya	„	1	2	0	1	4
4.	Sasibhushan Bhattacharyya	„	2	2	0	1	5
5.	Dwijapada Bhattacharyya	„	1	1	1	0	3
6.	Shankar. Ch. Bhattacharyya	„	1	1	0	0	2
7.	Gurudayal Bhandari	Barber	2	2	0	0	4
8.	Jatindranath Pal	Potter	1	2	0	0	3
9.	Bholanath Shaha	Weaver	1	1	2	0	4
10.	Dibakar Datta	„	0	1	1	0	2
11.	Kalidas Das	„	0	1	1	0	2
12.	Srimati Putu	Tambuli	0	2	0	0	2
13.	Surendranath Dom	Dom	1	1	1	2	5
14.	Pada Dom	„	1	1	0	0	2
15.	Radhi Dom	„	1	2	0	1	4
16.	Rakhahari Hadi	Hadi	1	3	0	0	4
17.	Hrishikesh Hadi	„	3	1	2	1	7
18.	Khudiram Bayen	Cobbler	1	3	0	1	5
19.	Rashik Bayen	„	1	1	2	0	4
20.	Dwarik Bayen	„	1	1	0	1	3
21.	Srimati Kumud	„	0	1	1	0	2
22.	Apal Bayen	„	1	2	1	0	4
23.	Panchanan Bayen	„	1	2	0	1	4
24.	Bhudhar Bayen	„	1	1	0	0	2
	Total——		24	35	13	12	84

Appendices.

Distribution of land.

Land held by each householder of the village.

	Name	Quantity of land	Union Board Tax
1.	Sridhar Bhattacharyya	30 biggahs	Rs. 1-12-0
2.	Panchanan Bhattacharyya ×	9 "	" 0-12-0
3.	Sambhunath Mukhopadhyaya	35 "	" 1-2-0
4.	Sasibhushan Bhattacharyya	30 "	" 1-8-0
5.	Dwijapada Bhattacharyya	15 "	" 1-2-0
6.	Shankarchandra Bhattacharyya	18 "	" 1 2-0
7.	Gurudayal Bhandari	×	×
8.	Jatindranath Pal	9 biggaha	" 0-12-0
9.	Bholanath Shaha	20 "	" 0-8-0
10.	Dibakar Datta	12 "	" 1-0-0
11.	Kalipada Das	10 "	" 0-9-0
12.	Srimati Putu	3 "	×
13.	Surendranath Dom	×	" 0-6-0
14.	Pada Dom	×	×
15.	Radhai Dom	×	×
16.	Rakhahari Hadi	×	×
17.	Hrishikesh Hadi	×	×
18.	Khudiram Bayen	20 biggahs	" 2-0 0
19.	Rashik Bayen	6 "	" 0 12-0
20.	Dwarik Bayen	1 biggah, 5 kattahs	×
21.	Srimati Kumud	14 "	" 1--8-0
22.	Apal Bayen	8 "	" 0-9-0
23.	Panchanan Bayen	25 kattahs	×
24.	Bhudar Bayen	4 biggahs "	" 0-6-0
	Total——	241 biggahs, 10 kattahs	Rs. 16-12-0

* Sj. Panchanan Bhattacharyya possesses one biggah of land in his own village and the other 8 biggahs in a separate village.

Appendices.

Population.

Castes		Families	Men	Women	Boys	Girls	Total Number of Inhabitants.
1.	Brahmin	6	7	7	2	5	21
2.	Weaver	3	1	3	4	0	8
3.	Potter	1	1	2	0	0	3
4.	Barber	1	2	2	0	0	4
5.	Tambuli	1	0	2	0	0	2
6.	Cobbler	7	6	11	4	3	24
7.	Hadi	2	4	4	2	1	11
8.	Dom	3	3	4	1	3	11
	Total——	24	24	35	13	12	84

Appendices.

Domestic Animals.

Bulls	2	Goats	40
Bullocks	36	Horse	0
Cows	77	Mare	0
Calves	50	Ponies	0
Buffaloes	0	Donkey	0
Sheep	0	Pigs	2

Plough

A plough has four parts (1) or (১) Rish (stem)—it is made of wood, and when good sal wood is used the price of a Rish will cost from 10as. to 12as ; when the wood is bad the cost is 4as. only. The length of a Rish is generally 3½ to 4 cubits. Rishes are used in the specified length because of the size of the oxen employed in drawing the plough. In case of using larger oxen and buffaloes for ploughing, the Rish has to be from 4½ to 5 cubits in length. That end of the Rish which is attached to the plough is 18 inches in circumference. From this end the Rish goes on becoming thinner to the other end which is twelve inches only in circumference. The Rish can be detached from the plough whenever necessary.

Plough

(2) or (২) is called *Phal* (plough-share)—it is made of iron and the local blacksmith makes it. The *Phal* may be of 2 kinds—(1) the thicker kind known as *Suno-Phal*, (2) the thinner kind, known as the *Goche-Phal.* The first kind is 12 inches long, 7½ inches broad, and costs 8as ; the second is 12 to 18 inches long, 2½ inches broad and costs 5as.

The breadth of the *Phal* means the measure of that part of it where it joins the plough. From this joint it ends tapering into a point. This can be seen in the picture. The *Phal* can be detached from the plough if necessary. and may be replaced when so needed. The ploughman can himself manipulate it. It has to be sharpened five times a year by a blacksmith, costing 5 pices each time.

The portion from the end of the share (phal) up to the handle marked (৩) is called the Plough (langal). A plough is generally made of jam-wood or babla-wood. A good plough made of babla-wood lasts about 15-16 years ; if it is carefully used it can go on for 30 to 40 years. A plough made of jam wood gives good use for 7—8 years. A plough costs 14 annas.

The portion marked (৬) is called the handle of the plough (bonta). The cultivators drive the plough by taking hold of it by the bonta. The cultivators use the word plough in two senses; —(a) the implement as a whole shown in the picture, or (b) the portion between the figures (২) and (৬)

Yoke.

The portion marked (১) is called the yoke. This has to be very light. For this reason it is made of very light wood such as the suckers of Banyan-tree ("ba" or "bo") and wood of mango, shisu and jiga (generally called jiol) and such other trees. A yoke is from 3½ to 4½ cubits long. The circumference of the middle portion is 22 inches, those of the two ends, 12 inches. The price of a yoke is 8as. to 14as.

Yoke

The portion marked (২) is called Gonj (peg) Every yoke has two pegs and these have been shown in the picture. A peg may be made of the thin end of a bamboo or of wood. It is 14 inches long. The middle part of the yoke is tied up with leathern thong made out of cow or buffalo hide which is called "*Phita*" (tape). It is called also *Aalam.*

The bent part marked (৩) is called Ankro or clasp ; it is made of tentul (tamarind) babla, shirish or orjun-wood. The piece of rope attached to the clasp is called the rope of the plough : it is made of jute and is 8-10 cubits long and 3 inches in circumference. A piece of rope of this kind costs 12 annas.

A yoke remains useful for 8-10 years.

Harrow

This ladder-like harrow is made of bamboo. It is 3½ cubits long and 12 inches broad. A piece of bamboo 3½ cubits long is split length wise into two halves and then a few rungs made of bamboo about I4

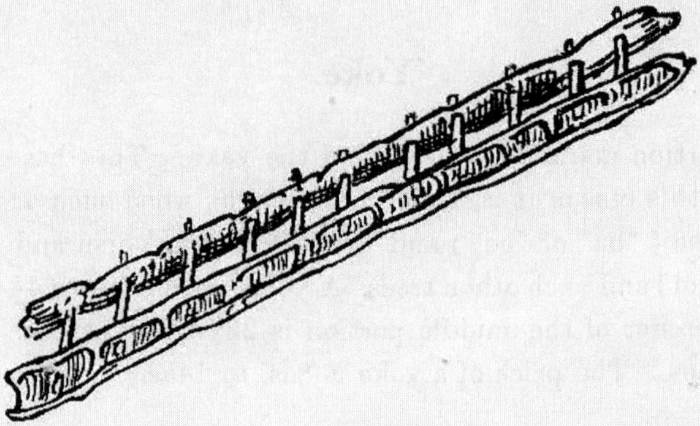

Harrow

inches in length are attached to these two pieces of split bamboo. The local carpenters make this harrow. It cost 8as and lasts for two years. This is used for levelling the ground when it is ploughed up for cultivation.

Spade

The length of a spade is 12 inches, the breadth 10 inches ; the local black-smith makes such spades. A spade costs Rs. 1-8-0. The householders themselves make wooden handles for spade.

After the land is ploughed it has to be bound with *"al"*s (raised alleys). For this spades are essential. A spade is also used for digging

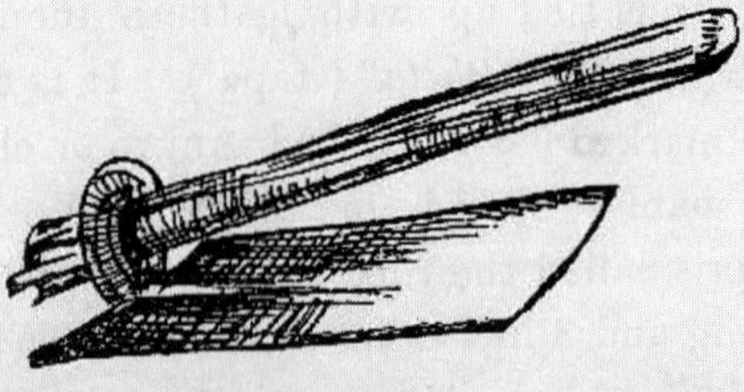

Spade

drains for the entrance and exit of water. In cultivating potato, sugar-cane, brinjal the spade is generally used.

Every year a spade has to be repaired by a black-smith costing about Rs. 1-4-0. When it is thus repaired every year, it may be used for 4-5 years.

Banti

(A large knife fixed to a seat).

A banti has two parts—the knife or the cutting part (da) and the seat (bant) or handle,

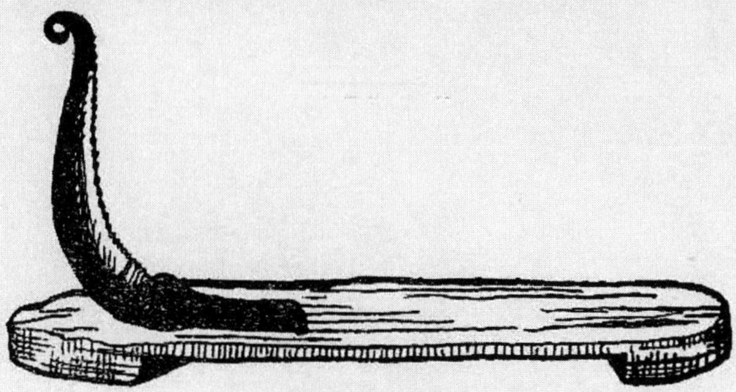

Banti

The knife of the banti stands 1 cubit high and is 2 inches broad ; it is sharp as a scythe. It costs 1 Re. together with the seat or the handle. It is used for cutting the straw into small pieces for the cattle. A banti may be used for 5 or 6 years and needs sharpening thrice every month. The charge for sharpening is about an anna.

Sickle.

The price of a Sickle is 4as. The handle is made of the thick wood of a mango-tree. Any other kind of wood does not make a good handle for a sickle. In the current language of the village it is called "*kede.*"

Sickle.

A sickle is used for reaping paddy, for thatching roofs, for cutting straw for the cow, for cutting grass and scraping sugar-cane stalks. A sickle lasts for 2-3 years. The cost of sharpening it every month is 6 pies.

Printed and Published by Rai Saheb Jagadananda Roy,
at the Santiniketan Press, Santiniketan, Birbhum.

Appendix II

Three Village Economic Studies on Rice

Visva-Bharati Rural Studies, Nos. 1, 2 and 3

THREE VILLAGE ECONOMIC STUDIES

ON

RICE

1. Thirty-Eight Years of Rice Yields.
2. Varieties and Yields of Rice in Benuria Mauza.
3. The Rice Industry in Lower Birbhum.

विश्वभारती शान्तिनिकेतन

BY

HASHIM AMIR ALI, Ph.D. (Cornell)

Assisted by

TARA KRISHNA BASU, B.A. (Hons.)

AND

JITENDRANATH TALUKDAR

MAY, 1934

Price Re. 1

Visva-Bharati Rural Studies, No. 1

THIRTY-EIGHT YEARS

OF

RICE YIELDS

IN LOWER BIRBHUM, BENGAL

BY

HASHIM AMIR ALI, Ph.D. (Cornell)

Assisted by

TARA KRISHNA BOSE, B.A. (Hons.)

AND

JITENDRANATH TALUKDAR

These studies are dedicated to Leonard K. Elmhirst, the first Director of Sriniketan, and his wife, Dorothy Elmhirst, both of whom have been patient, true and generous friends of India and her rural population.

PREFACE

These three village economic studies on rice are being published together because they give a composite economic analysis of an agricultural industry which is of considerable importance in many parts of India.

The first two are reprinted by the kind permission of the Editor, Prof. P. C. Mahalanobis from *Sankhya,* the Indian Journal of Statistics, Vol. 1, Part 4, 1934, and I am deeply obliged to him not only for many valuable suggestions but for some statistical calculations and editorial help as well.

The third and last pertaining to the rice industry and its effects on local economy is really a problem in village economics taken up and worked out with much labour by my student and colleague, Tara Krishna Basu ; my only contributions to it consist of suggestions from time to time and the final writing up after he had laboriously collected the data. My obligation to him and his fellow student, Jitendranath Talukdar, in the working out of the other studies also is considerable, while it must be mentioned that these studies would have been impossible if it were not for the ready assistance given by many people in the villages, notable amongst whom are Sjts. Jagat Bandhu Pal, Zamindar of Bahadurpur, Sachindranath Mukherjee, M.Sc., Vice-President of Bolpur Union Board, Mohammad Mondal of Lohagarh, Binode Pal of Islampur and Pathu Mukerjee of Bahadurpur.

These studies should be of considerable help to any agency attempting rural reconstruction in the region dealt with : but the purpose with which so much labour has been put in them will not have been served if they do not give rise to and help in similar studies in other parts of India also. They are such as to be possible and useful anywhere provided attempts are made to get similar data, and until such studies *dealing with actual village conditions* are forthcoming in large numbers it is impossible to formulate a policy of agricultural and economic development that will really bring about practical results.

H. A. A.

SANTINIKETAN,
May, 1934.

CONTENTS

THIRTY-EIGHT YEARS OF RICE YIELDS IN LOWER BIRBHUM, BENGAL*

By HASHIM AMIR ALI, Ph.D., Assisted by TARA KRISHNA BOSE, B.A.,
Visva-Bharati Institute of Rural Reconstruction, Sriniketan, Bengal.

Introduction.

Rice is easily the most important crop in Bengal, no less than about 20 million acres out of a total cultivated area of about 23 million acres being under this crop alone, but reliable records of yields extending over 30 or 40 years are extremely rare. In the present paper have been given the yield data for 38 years beginning from the crop season of 1894 for a number of plots situated in the village of Bahadurpur (lat. 23°40′ N, long. 87°40′ E approximately) in the district of Birbhum in Bengal. The village lies within a couple of miles of Bolpur station on the East Indian Railway at a distance of 99 miles from Calcutta. It is situated within the intensive area of village reconstruction work sponsored by Rabindranath Tagore's Visva-Bharati Institute of Rural Reconstruction.

The material was collected from the manuscript records of Mr. Jagatbandhu Pal, a local *zamindar* (land-owner) to whom we are grateful for kindly lending them to us. A part of the contents were in Mr. Pal's hand and dated back to the year 1301 Bengali era (1893-94 A.D.). As far as I know, there are no published figures for any farm in Bengal which date so far back. The great majority of Government farms have been opened later, but even where earlier figures are available they give the yields of crops grown under special conditions. But here the figures refer directly to village plots, and since the interests of both landlord and tenant (both of whom were generally present at the time) were involved in the measurements, they were not likely to be distinctly partial one way or the other.

All the figures were taken from two registers and a few loose sheets that were pinned on to the pages of these registers. The figures were all in Bengali and an exact translation of the same for one year (1902 A.D.) has been given in the Appendix. Just what those figures represent is this:

The local zamindar Babu Jagatbandhu Pal has many plots of land scattered in and about Bahadurpur village and elsewhere. These plots are uniformly scattered over all the land of the village. Out of the lands in Bahadurpur itself, he cultivated during this year (1902) 25·2 *bighas*[1] under his direct supervision paying the wages in cash. Besides, he gave out 4·4 bighas either on *krishān* or on *borgā* systems, *i.e.*, he merely rented the use

*Reprinted from *Sankhyā*, Vol. 1, Part 4, October, 1934, by kind permission of the Editor, Prof. P. C. Mahalanobis.

1. The village table for measurements of area :—

45 sq. ft.	= 1 *chatāk*	=	5 sq. yds.	=	0·001033 acre
16 *chatāks*	= 1 *kāthā*	=	80 sq. yds.	=	0·016529 acre
20 *kāthās*	= 1 *bighā*	=	1,600 sq. yds.	=	0·330579 acre

TABLE 1.—YIELD OF PADDY AND STRAW IN BAHADURPUR VILLAGE.

YEAR		YIELD OF A SINGLE PLOT S		YIELD OF PLOTS D (CULTIVATED BY OWNER)						
				PADDY AND STRAW				PADDY ONLY		
Bengali Era	A.D.	Paddy Mds. per bigha	Straw bundles	No. of Plots	Area (bigha)	Paddy mds. per bigha	Straw bundles	No. of Plots	Area (bigha)	Paddy Mds. per bigha
(1)	(2)	(3)	(4)	(5)	(6)	(7)	(8)	(9)	(10)	(11)
1301	1894	3·9	640	13	14·2	7·2	580	5	8·4	5·6
02	95	6·5	600	9	10·7	4·2	480	7	15·0	1·8
03	96	8·0	880	8	7·4	3·0	440	3	3·1	2·3
04	97	9·6	860	10	9·2	7·5	620	14	19·5	7·8
05	98	10·2	710	15	16·4	10·3	960	10	13·0	9·4
06	99	11·3	650	9	7·0	7·2	640	10	20·5	6·7
07	1900	5·0	300	3	1·5	2·4	280	5	2·9	5·6
08	01	9·5	800	12	11·2	8·1	680	9	12·0	7·6
09	02	9·1	780	9	8·3	6·2	680	13	16·9	6·4
1310	03	5·1	330	8	6·3	2·6	280	7	12·2	3·3
11	04	8·7	1000	2	0·8	7·4	180	15	17·7	6·9
12	05	5·5	600	8	9·2	5·2	500	17	19·1	8·6
13	06	8·4	1100	3	1·9	7·6	720	11	15·2	4·6
14	07	7·8	800	5	4·3	7·2	800	19	24·4	4·6
15	08	9·4	890	13	13·1	8·9	880	9	11·9	9·7
16	09	5·6	600	7	3·2	5·5	560	6	7·7	4·3
17	1910	6·7	650	12	12·2	8·0	600	14	16·6	5·8
18	11	5·9	600	12	11·6	9·2	780	16	18·4	10·0
19	12	3·6	440	13	11·5	2·8	620	7	9·0	2·5
1320	13	8·0	700	15	11·8	8·2	880	9	15·4	9·3
21	14	3·0	600	6	7·0	6·5	820	14	19.3	6·6
22	15	...	...	5	4·2	2·7	400	8	14·3	0·8
23	16	10·7	800	11	10·2	6·2	600	9	25·6	4·2
24	17	8·1	800	11	8·3	8·0	920	16	23·2	9·0
25	18	11·3	900	4	2·3	7·2	940	22	28·8	6·7
26	19	7·4	...	...	...	...	...	10	5·6	6·2
27	1920	5·9	...	...	...	...	...	33	41·4	4·0
28	21	9·3	...	...	...	...	...	29	49·7	6·0
29	22	11·3	1000	11	13·1	11·6	1000	26	33·7	11·2
1330	23	8·8	750	12	11·5	8·0	760	23	36·9	8·3
31	24	6·3	850	10	10·3	6·9	500	20	36·5	7·1
32	25	...	520	9	10·0	5·6	540	20	30·1	5·9
33	26	6·2	490	9	9·3	5·4	640	19	39·9	5·5
34	27	4·0	400	33	49·0	4·0	480	...	...	4·0
35	28	6·4	400	42	48·1	10·2	1060	...	...	10·2
36	29	7·6	680	17	19·7	6·9	700	19	39·9	3·4
37	30	9·7	640	19	21·3	10·5	780	22	43·2	3·3
38	31	...	680	15	23·0	7·3	580	17	23·4	6·8
TOTAL or average	..	7·5	986	400	419·1	6·9	6·73	513	770·7	6·1

TABLE 1.—YIELD OF PADDY AND STRAW IN BAHADURPUR VILLAGE

YEAR		YIELD OF PLOTS B (SHARE SYSTEM)			YIELD OF ALL PLOTS (OWNER-CULTIVATED AND SHARE SYSTEM)				
Bengali Era	A.D.	No. of Plots	Area (bigha)	Paddy mds. per bigha	No. of Plots	Total area		Yield of paddy	
						in bigha	in acres	Mds. per bigha	lbs. per acre
(1)	(2)	(12)	(13)	(14)	(15)	(16)	(17)	(18)	(19)
1301	1894	...	...	...	18	22·6	7·47	6·3	1571
02	95	...	...	...	16	25·7	8·50	2·8	698
03	96	...	...	...	11	10·5	3·47	1·4	349
04	97	...	...	.	24	28·7	9·49	7·6	1895
05	98	...	...	...	25	29·4	9·72	9·9	2469
06	99	...	...	...	19	27·5	9·09	6·8	1596
07	1900	...	...	..	8	4·4	1·45	4·5	1122
08	01	5	9·2	5·2	26	33·4	11·04	5·6	1396
09	02	5	4·4	8·4	27	29·6	9·78	6·6	1646
1310	03	3	2·5	2·6	18	20·9	6·91	3·1	773
11	04	22	38·1	4·5	39	56·6	18·71	4·9	1222
12	05	..	(37·1)†	...	25	28·4	9·39	7·4	1845
13	06	17	36·1	4·2	31	53·7	17·75	4·5	1122
14	07	7	9·6	4·4	31	38·3	12·66	4·8	1197
15	08	28	42·9	6·6	50	67·9	22·45	7·6	1895
16	09	24	39·6	2·4	37	50·6	16·73	3·1	773
17	1910	...	(42·4)†	...	26	28·8	9·52	6·7	1671
18	11	25	45·2	5·1	53	75·2	24·86	6·9	1721
19	12	15	30·8	2·1	35	51·8	17·12	2·3	573
1320	13	23	49·0	7·2	47	76·2	25·19	7·7	2000
21	14	22	44·2	4·2	42	70·5	23·31	5·1	1272
22	15	...	(33·8)†	..	13	18·5	6·12	1·2	299
23	16	17	22·8	4·3	37	58·6	19·37	4·6	1147
24	17	23	20·2	6·1	50	51·5	17·02	7·7	1920
25	18	21	31·3	2·7	47	62·4	20·63	3·5	873
26	19	...	(38·5)†	...	10	5·6	1·85	6·2	1546
27	1920	26	45·8	2·3	59	87·2	28·83	3·1	773
28	21	27	29·7	3·2	56	79·3	26·21	4·9	1222
29	22	29	29·4	6·9	6	76·2	25·19	9·3	2319
1330	23	31	39·2	4·6	6	87·6	28·96	6·6	1646
31	24	20	18·9	4·2	50	65·7	21·72	6·2	1546
32	25	11	21·4	3·6	40	61·5	20·33	5·1	1272
33	26	22	34·5	3·5	50	83·5	27·60	4·6	1147
34	27	6	20·3	1·3	39	69·2	22·88	3·5	873
35	28	30	52·5	4·2	72	100·5	33·22	8·1	2020
36	29	21	23·2	4·6	57	82·8	27·37	4·8	1197
37	1930	19	26·4	6·2	60	89·8	29·69	4·8	1197
38	31	32	87·5	3·4	64	133·9	44·26	5·2	1297
TOTAL ..	...	531	854·7	...	1444	2044·5	...	...	...

† Figures within brackets are interpolated values used for filling gaps in the data

of the land in exchange for varying returns from the cultivator according to the exact terms of the transaction in each case.

At harvest time, both these classes of cultivators brought in the paddy and straw from their respective fields and stocked them in the large inner courtyard of the zamindar. Each of these heaps consisted of paddy from a group of plots either situated together or scattered around the village. In some cases there might be only one plot ; in others, several ; but, all that was written down was the area which each group consisted of. Then, each of these heaps were measured by a standard of village measure, consisting either of a basket or a vessel made out of metal, known as the *soli*[2] and the fractions left over were measured in *seers*[2] and *chatāks*[2].

The fifth figure (see Appendix), for example, shows that in one group of plots (situated together or scattered) consisting together of 2 bighas 17 kathas of land, the yield that year was 4 maaps—5 solis—17 seers—4 chataks. In this case nothing else was mentioned as to the identity of the plots. In one year a group might consist of ten plots ; in the next year the ten plots might be cultivated by different persons and so on. And figures like this were available for 38 years.

The first thing to do was to reduce all the figures of area as well as yields to standard units of measurements.[3] This involved the conversion of some three thousand figures from one system of measures to another. The next step was to see if any individual plots were consistently mentioned throughout the period, and after an elaborate system of classification it was found that there were two units of area, one of 8 kathas (about 0·125 acres) and another of 16 kathas (about 0·25 acres) the first of which recurred in all but three years, while the second was mentioned for about half the number of years. Now this area of 8 kathas is too small to consist of more than one plot ; and later the plot was actually identified.

Thus we got four sets of figures that will be found in Table 1 :—

(1) The figures for one single plot (referred to as Plot S) giving the yields of paddy and of straw from year to year.

(2) The figures for the plots (Plots D) cultivated under the direct supervision of the zamindar for some of which yields of straw were also noted.

(3) The figures for the plots given out on borgā (Plots B) which meant that only the paddy was to be shared between the zamindar and the cultivator in the ratio of 22 to 18 or thereabout ; while the straw went generally to the tenant. In this case, therefore, the yields of paddy alone were recorded.

(4) The average yields per bigha of all the plots, whether cultivated under the zamindar's supervision or by being leased out on the borgā system (col. 15, 16, 17 in Table 1).

---

[2] The village table for measurement of volume is as follows :—

16 village *chatāks*	... = 1 village *seer*	... =	1·46 lbs.	(of paddy)
20 ,, *seers*	... = 1 *solī*	... =	29·28 lbs.	(,,)
8 *solis*	... = 1 *māāp*	... =	234·23 lbs.	(,,)

[3] One *maund* = 82·286 lbs.

One *maund* per *bighā* = 248·915 lbs. per acre.

Variations in the Yield of Paddy.

Yield of the Individual Plot S. This plot as has been already mentioned consists only of about 8 kathas or about an eighth of an acre. The yields of paddy for all but 3 years since 1894 are given, and these are seen to vary considerably from year to year. The minimum was 3 maunds per bigha (747 lbs. per acre) in 1914, while the maximum of 11·3 mds. per bigha (2813 lb. per acre) was reached in three years 1899, 1918 and 1922. The mean yield is 7·6 mds. per bigha (1892 lbs. per acre) with a standard deviation of 2·4 mds. (597 lbs.). In view of the excessive short period fluctuations, and the small number of readings, no significant trend can be expected that will denote an improvement or decline in the fertility of the plot during the past 38 years.

Similarly, although the figures are seen to be rough estimates only, the mean yield of straw works out to be 686·9 bundles per bigha, with a standard deviation of 113·4.

As we shall see later the mean yield of paddy for this plot is considerably higher than the mean obtained from the paddy yield of all the plots taken together. But with regard to the yield of straw it might here be noted that the mean obtained for the yield of straw from other plots does not differ much.

The mean yields of paddy for different groups (weighted averages from total area*) are given below.

Table 2. Mean Yield of Paddy under Different Cultivation

Cultivation Arrangements	n	Yield of paddy (in maunds per bigha)		Yield of paddy (in lbs. per acre)	
		Mean ± P.E.	S.D. ± P.E.	Mean ± P.E.	S.D. ± P.E.
1. Plots cultivated under direct supervision	913	6·52 ± 0·30	2·74 ± 0·21	1623 ± 75	682 ± 58
2. Plots cultivated by tenants on *borgā* or *krishani* system ...	531	4·27 ± 0·17	1·53 ± 0·12	1063 ± 42	381 ± 29
3. Average of all plots	1444	5·40 ± 0·19	1·76 ± 0·14	1344 ± 48	438 ± 34

The difference between the mean yield under direct cultivation 6·52±0·30 mds. per bigha (1623±75 lbs. per acre) and the mean yield under the tenancy system 4·27±0·17 mds. per bigha (1063±42 lbs. per acre) is noteworthy. The mean yield of the former is practically one and a half times greater than the mean yield under the share system.

What then does this signify? It can only mean that one or both of the following two conditions exist. Either the land given out to tenants is generally poorer and less fertile, so that given the same amount of care and cultivation the yield remains low; or it might mean that the tenant being poor and less equipped is unable to give as much attention to the cultivation of the land as the landowner himself. Probably both these causes operate with the result that the agricultural industry as a whole becomes less and less efficient and the peasants more and more impoverished.

The Trend-line for Yield of Paddy.

Finally we may make a joint analysis of all the readings pertaining to the yield of paddy from year to year since 1894. The number of readings amount to no less than 1,444 and they refer to an aggregate of 2,043.6 bighas (675.6 acres).

*See Editorial Note on p. 17

The first question is: Is there a trend? Can we find any general increase or decrease in the fertility as shown in the yields obtained from year to year?

If the figures show even a slightly downward trend, they would substantiate the claims of some agricultural economists who contend that due to improper manuring and careless cultivation the soil of India was being impoverished. In that case the evident remedy to be suggested would be proper manuring. If, on the other hand, they show a slightly upward trend, we might rejoice at both the destruction of a pessimistic theory as well as at the gradual progress that we might expect in agriculture. Lastly, if the trend obtained is no more than a straight line more or less horizontal, well then even that would give us a scientific basis for asserting that the yield per acre has been at a constant level at least for the last forty years.

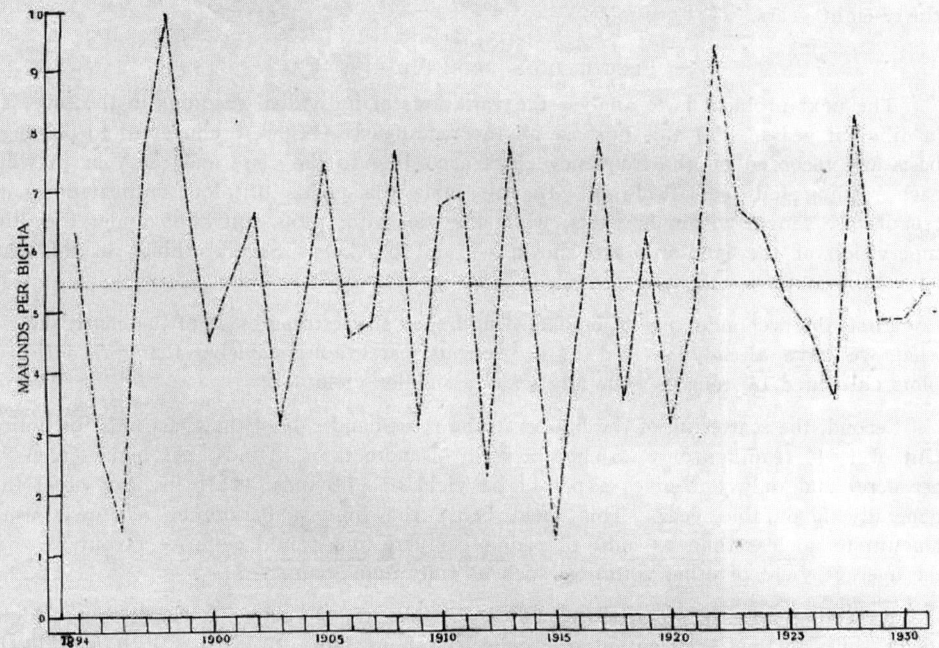

CHART I. RICE-YIELDS FOR 38 YEARS

I am indebted to Prof. P. C. Mahalanobis of the Statistical Laboratory, Presidency College, Calcutta, for supplying me with the following trend or straight line of best fit.*

$$Y = 5{\cdot}40 - 0{\cdot}0016\,(t - 1913) \quad \ldots \quad \ldots \quad (1)$$

where y = Yield of paddy in maunds per bigha and t = Year.

The mean yield of rice during the period 1894-1930 was 5.40 mds. per bigha (1344 lbs. per acre). The annual yield varied from 1.2 mds. per bigha (299 lbs. per acre) in 1915 to 9.9 mds. per bigha (2,464 lbs. per acre) in 1898. The observed values of the annual yields together with the trend-line are shown in Chart I.

*See Editorial Note No. 1 on p. 17.

It will be noticed that the trend-line is practically horizontal which shows that there was no steady change in the average yield during this period. In fact the regression coefficient −0·0016 (which represents a decrease in yield of a little over half a seer per bigha or less than half a pound per acre in ten years) is statistically insignificant.

It is clear, therefore, that as far as the figures analysed are concerned there seems to be no tendency either upward or downward in the general fertility of the soil under consideration. The variations from year to year are likely to have been caused by other factors such as rainfall, manurial treatment, health, intensity of cultivation etc. The soil is either not capable of producing a generally higher yield, or through the cultivation of centuries it has reached the lowest level of fertility. Which of these possibilities holds ground and what the annual fluctuations are due to we shall consider later. But, in any case, there has been no appreciable change in the fertility of the soil for the last thirty-eight years.

Fluctuations from Year to Year.

The next problem is to analyse the variations of individual readings in the same and in different years. For this purpose all the readings (1,444) were converted to per bigha basis and recorded on the frequency chart according to the class and the year in which each reading fell (see Table 3). In this table the yields of plots cultivated by the tenants are shown within brackets, while the yields for plots cultivated under the direct supervision of the landlords are shown without brackets. Several things in this chart have to be noted :—

First, the preponderance of bracketed figures in the left-hand side of the chart, showing what we have already noticed in a previous paragraph, namely, that the yields of plots cultivated by tenants generally show a smaller yield.

Second, the scattering of the figures in the right-hand side of the chart must be noticed Out of 1,444 readings only 25 show a yield of more than 13 mds. per bigha (3236 lbs. per acre) and only one gives a per bigha yield of 17·8 mds. (4431 lbs. per acre) in a generally favourable year. This yield being the highest maximum recorded, would amount to no less than 53 mds. of paddy per acre and would compare favourably with the average yield of other countries such as Italy and Spain.†

Expecting some light to be thrown on the problem of factors determining the higher yields some further information was collected about these 22 plots. With considerable difficulty they were indentified from the records of the zamindar, and their location was plotted. It was found that the more fertile plots are generally situated in the lower lands of the village, but are not confined to a series of adjacent plots. One of these plots has given a yield of more than 13 mds. per bigha (3236 lbs. per acre) three times during the last 38 years. Another has given such a yield twice, and the rest only once each. By far the majority of them have been cultivated by the owner himself with hired labour, and it is interesting to note that apart from our study the owner is already aware of the fact that these plots are more fertile than the others, and explains that this is because these lands have been in the possession of the family for a long time and that the residual effect of large amounts of manure given in past years is the basis of their greater fertility. It is impossible, however, to test this hypothesis for want of sufficient data.

---

†See *Varieties and Yields of Rice in Benuria Mauza*, Table 3, *Sankhyā*, p. 369.

TABLE 3.—FREQUENCY CHART FOR YIELD OF PADDY

Year	Yield in Maunds per Bigha																		Total Number of Plots	
	1	2	3	4	5	6	7	8	9	10	11	12	13	14	15	16	17	18	Owner-Cultivated	Share System
1894	—	—	—	1	—	2	3	7	5	—	—	—	—	—	—	—	—	—	18	—
1895	—	3	4	4		2	3	—	—	—	—	—	—	—	—	—	—	...	16	—
1896	3	—	1	2	1	1	1	2	—	—	—	—	—	—	—	—	—	—	11	—
1897	—	—	—	—	—	—	6	9	5	3	—	—	—	1	—	—	—	—	24	—
1898	—	—	—	—	—	—	1	2	3	3	4	7	4	1	—	—	—	—	25	—
1899	—	—	—	—	1	1	7	3	1	3	3	—	—	—	—	—	—	—	19	—
1900	—	1	2	2	1	—	1	1	—	—	—	—	—	—	—	—	—	—	8	—
1901	—	—	—	(1) 1	(2) —	(1) 2	(1) 2	3	4	4	2	1	2	—	—	—	—	—	21	5
1902	—	—	—	—	3	(3) 6	(1) 2	6	—	4	—	—	—	(1) —	—	—	1	—	22	5
1903	—	1	1	(1) 1	(1) 7	4	—	1	—	(1) —	—	—	—	—	—	—	—	—	15	3
1904	(1) —	(1) —	(4) —	(3) —	(1) 3	1	(10) 3	(2) 5	1	2	1	1	—	—	—	—	—	—	17	22
1905	—	—	—	1	3	7	6	3	5	—	—	—	—	—	—	—	—	—	25	—
1906	(1) —	(1) —	(2) —	(3) 2	(3) 2	(5) 2	(2) 2	3	2	—	—	—	—	—	—	—	—	1	14	17
1907	—	—	(2) 1	7	(1) 4	(3) 7	(1) —	2	3	—	—	—	—	—	—	—	—	—	24	7
1908	—	—	(1) —	(4) —	(4) —	(5) —	(3) 1	(4) 3	(1) 6	(5) 2	(1) 3	2	4	1	—	—	—	—	22	28
1909	(2) —	(8) —	(5) 1	(4) 3	(4) 4	2	2	—	(1, —	—	—	—	—	—	1	—	—	—	13	24
1910	—	3	2	—	2	1	4	4	7	1	1	1	—	—	—	—	—	—	26	—
1911	—	(1) —	(3) —	(2) —	(7) —	(4) 3	(2) 1	(3) 3	(1) 1	4	(1) 8	1	4	(1) —	1	2	—	—	28	25
1912	(3) 2	(4) 4	(1) 5	(1) 6	(2) —	(2) 1	1	(1) 1	—	(1) —	—	--	—	—	—	—	—	—	20	15
1913	—	--	(1) —	(2) 1	(3) —	(2) —	(3) 4	(2) 4	(3) 5	(2) 1	(1) 3	(4) 2	2	1	—	1	—	—	24	23
1914	(1) —	1	(4) —	1	(2) 3	(3) 1	(4) 5	(7) 2	(1) 7	—	—	—	—	—	—	—	—	—	20	22

TABLE 8.—FREQUENCY CHART FOR YIELD OF PADDY—*Contd.*

Year	Yield in Maunds per Bigha																		Total Number of Plots	
	1	2	3	4	5	6	7	8	9	10	11	12	13	14	15	16	17	18	Owner-Cultivated	Share System
1915	7	1	3	2	—	—	—	—	—	—	—	—	—	—	—	—	—	—	13	—
1916	(1) —	(2) 2	(4) 3	(4) —	(3) 1	(0) 1	(1) 3	(1) 3	3	2	(1) 1	—	1	—	—	—	—	—	20	17
1917	—	—	—	(3) —	(2) —	(3) 1	(6) 1	(4) 7	(2) 7	(2) 7	(1) 2	—	1	—	—	1	—	—	27	23
1918	(1) —	(8) —	(2) —	(2) 1	(3) 5	(3) 3	(2) 3	6	4	1	2	1	—	—	—	—	—	—	26	21
1919	—	1	—	—	1	2	1	3	2	—	—	—	—	—	—	—	—	—	10	—
1920	(2) 1	(9) 3	(8) 6	(5) 5	2	(1) 5	3	5	1	(1) 1	1	—	—	—	—	—	—	—	33	26
1921	(2) —	(2) —	(4) 2	(12) 2	(4) 3	(2) 5	(1) 5	6	4	2	—	—	—	—	—	—	—	—	29	27
1922	—	1	(1) —	(3) —	(4) 1	(3) 1	(8) 1	(3) 2	(2) 2	(4) 4	(1) 6	8	5	3	1	1	—	1	37	29
1923	(1) —	(2) 1	(2) —	(10) —	(7) —	(3) 4	(4) 4	(2) 7	8	9	2	—	—	—	—	—	—	—	35	31
1924	—	(2) —	(6) 1	(2) 1	(3) 1	(2) 5	(3) 3	(1) 5	9	(1) 1	1	3	—	—	—	—	—	—	30	20
1925	—	1	(2) 1	(4) 1	(2) 3	(2) 6	(1) 6	7	2	—	1	1	—	—	—	—	—	—	29	11
1926	—	(7) —	(3) 1	(2) 5	(6) 2	(4) 6	4	5	1	2	—	2	—	—	—	—	—	—	28	22
1927	2	(6) —	4	5	9	5	2	2	3	—	—	—	—	—	—	—	—	1	33	6
1928	—	(2) —	(5) —	(5) —	(8) —	(4) —	(3) 3	(1) 3	(1) 5	14	(1) 5	4	7	—	1	—	—	—	42	30
1929	—	(1) —	(1) 3	(8) —	(3) 1	(3) 5	(4) 10	4	(1) 5	4	3	—	1	—	—	—	—	—	36	21
1930	—	—	(1) 1	(3) 1	1	(4) 1	(4) 1	(4) 4	(2) 6	12	9	(1) 2	1	2	—	—	—	—	41	19
1931	—	(2) —	(5) —	(4) 1	(9) 5	(4) 5	(3) 2	(3) 7	6	3	2	(1) 1	—	—	(1) —	—	—	—	32	32
Total (Owner-Cultivated)—	15	23	42	56	69	98	107	140	123	89	60	37	32	9	4	5	1	3	913	...
Total (Share System)	15	58	67	88	84	66	67	38	15	17	7	6	...	2	1	...	...	..	...	531
Grand Total	30	81	109	144	153	164	174	178	138	86	67	43	32	11	5	5	1	3		1444

Variations in the Area under Cultivation.

The fluctuations in the total area cultivated are also very large. In one year, for example, the yield of 62 bighas have been recorded ; in the very next year the yield of not more than 5·6 bighas have been noted. The decrease in the area was stated by the owner to have been caused by lack of rains in the early part of the season, which prevented much of the land from being taken up for cultivation during these years.

In spite of these fluctuations, however, there is a general upward tendency in the total number of bighas for which yields have been recorded in different years ; and to ascertain the cause of this tendency the figures were analysed in more detail.

Table 4.—Five Years' Moving Average of Area under Cultivation

Year		Area in Bighas		
Bengali Era	A. D.	Share System (Table 1, Col. 13)	Owner-Cultivated (Table 1, Col. 6+10)	Total Area
(1)	(2)	(3)	(4)	(5)
1301−05	1894−98	..	11·7	23·4
−06	−99	...	12·2	24·4
−07	−1900	...	10·0	20·1
−08	−01	...	11·4	24·7
−09	−02	...	11·0	24·9
−10	−03	...	9·9	23·2
−11	−04	...	9·0	29·0
−12	−05	18·3	11·4	33·8
−13	−06	27·3	10·8	37·9
−14	−07	24·7	11·1	39·6
−15	−08	32·8	11·8	49·0
−16	−09	33·1	11·2	47·8
−17	−10	34·1	11·3	47·9
−18	−11	35·9	12·6	52·2
−19	−12	40·2	11·7	54·9
−20	−13	41·4	12·0	56·5
−21	−14	42·3	13·5	60·5
−22	−15	40·6	12·5	58·5
−23	−16	36·1	13·0	55·1
−24	−17	34·0	14·2	55·1
−25	−18	30·5	14·5	52·3
−26	−19	29·3	19·5*	39·3
−27	−20	31·7	24·9*	53·1
−28	−21	33·1	28·9*	57·2
−29	−22	36·7	31·0*	62·1
−30	−23	38·3	32·7*	67·2
−31	−24	34·4	38·8*	79·2
−32	−25	27·7	36·6	74·1
−33	−26	28·7	23·1	74·9
−34	−27	25·1	18·0*	73·5
−35	−28	27·7	25·3*	76·1
−36	−29	28·6	27·2*	79·5
−37	−30	31·4	29·5*	85·2
−33	−31	37·4	32·2*	95·2

The figures available are shown in three curves obtained from 5 years moving averages given in Table 4 and illustrated in Chart 2.* The upper curve representing the total

*In calculating moving averages, gaps in the data have been filled up by the mean value of two contiguous figures. Records for Paddy and Straw (Table 1, Col. 6) missing for 1919-21, and for Paddy (Table 1, Col. 10) missing for 1927-28.

number of bighas shows that the zamindar had been recording the yields of more and more land during this period. But whether the increase is due to more and more virgin soil being brought under cultivation or due to his acquiring more and more land that was already under cultivation it is difficult to say. Probably the latter surmise comes nearer to the truth. In fact that is the explanation given by the zamindar himself.

The two lower curves show the number of bighas cultivated from year to year under direct supervision and on borga respectively. And the differenc between the two curves needs to be noted. The land cultivated by hired labour shows a steady rise while even the five years' averages pertaining to land given on borga show heavy fluctuations and no definite rise.

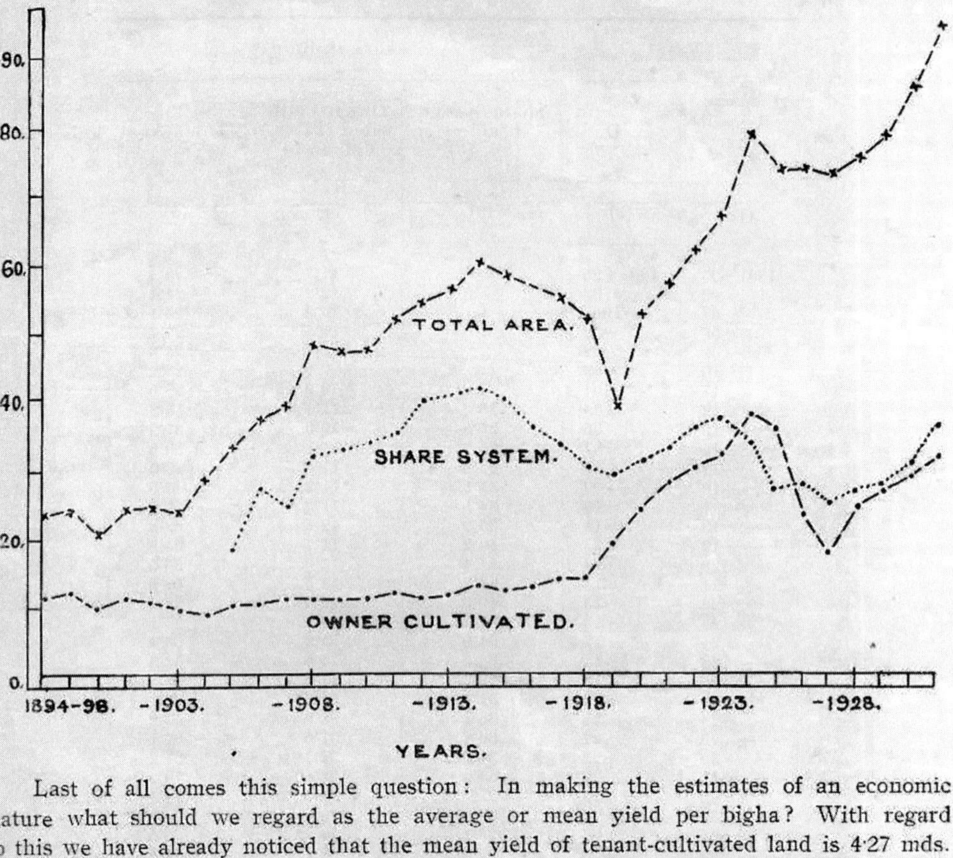

Last of all comes this simple question: In making the estimates of an economic nature what should we regard as the average or mean yield per bigha? With regard to this we have already noticed that the mean yield of tenant-cultivated land is 4·27 mds. per bigha (1063 lbs. per acre), that of zamindar-cultivated land is approximately 6·52 per bigha (1623 lbs. per acre), while the combined average yield is 5·40 mds. per bigha (1344 lbs. per acre).

The cause of this too was investigated and it appears probable that the rise in the case of land directly cultivated may be ascribed to the steady rise in the price of paddy for all but the last three years. When the price of paddy is on the rise it is more profitable for the owner of the land to pay the labourers in cash. On the other hand when the prices are low, the landlord would rather pay in kind, *i.e.*, give out the land on the share system. That is why more and more land was cultivated by hired labour during the past years. It is probably to be expected that with the present decline in prices this upward tendency of the area under direct cultivation will be considerably checked, and the amount of land cultivated on the share system will increase accordingly.

Combining this fact with what has been said before about the influence of a bad distribution of rainfall in the earlier part of the cultivation season, one might also surmise that it is the borga cultivated land that suffers most, while the cultivation of land by hired labour goes on even if the distribution of rainfall in the earlier part of the season is somewhat unfavourable. It is probably this factor which is responsible for the more pronounced fluctuations in the lowest curve which represents the area under the share system.

TABLE 5.—RAINFALL, ECONOMIC AND HEALTH DATA FOR THE REGION OF BAHADURPUR

YEAR		RAINFALL AT BOLPUR (in Inches)					HEALTH				
							BIRBHUM DISTRICT		BAHADUR-PUR VILLAGE	BOLPUR THANA	
Bengali Era	A.D.	June	July	August	Sept.	Total seasonal	Fever deaths	Excess of births over deaths	Total deaths	Total deaths	Fever deaths
(1)	(2)	(3)	(4)	(5)	(6)	(7)	(8)	(9)	(10)	(11)	(12)
1301	1894	11·43	11·74	10·55	9·84	43·56	24·9	3·46	—	—	—
1302	1895	8·52	7·62	5·82	6·46	28·42	23·8	3·06	—	—	—
1303	1896	10·50	12·77	10·62	9·16	43·05	23·4	4·27	—	—	—
1304	1897	6·35	7·95	10·22	8·90	33·42	19·6	10·43	—	—	—
1305	1898	13·60	10·17	15·49	9·77	49·03	14·3	18·57	—	—	—
1306	1899	10·98	12·77	9·16	10·62	43·53	16·8	18·70	—	—	—
1307	1900	7·08	6·59	7·83	19·75	41·25	19·0	12·57	—	—	—
1308	1901	7·36	11·01	7·13	10·94	36·44	17·9	12·54	—	—	—
1309	1902	2·88	11·29	7·18	8·20	29·55	19·5	11·36	5	—	—
1310	1903	7·67	3·11	13·83	8.64	33·25	19·5	3·80	4	2432	1672
1311	1904	9·88	18·73	10·54	4·12	43·27	20·4	11·77	...	2296	1520
1312	1905	3·69	20·29	13·76	10·39	48·13	25·4	1·15	17	—	—
1313	1906	5·41	14·92	15·96	4·59	40·88	29·9	9·23	25	4188	3234
1314	1907	10·00	9·75	6·64	8·78	35·17	38·3	26·00	11	4720	3794
1315	1908	17·38	16·70	10·63	6·82	51·53	33·5	20·13	15	4073	2737
1316	1909	8·53	4·64	26·73	7·66	47·56	23·0	6·10	4	2788	2174
1317	1910	12·19	10·35	8·89	6·09	37·52	22·6	12·38	11	2049	1907
1318	1911	13·15	14·34	22·76	1·95	52·20	24·0	7·68	19	2782	2108
1319	1912	—	0·52	8·71	2·96	12·19	28·9	6·19	13	3484	2778
1320	1913	16·27	11·60	14·23	4·50	47·05	27·4	2·78	13	2648	2248
1321	1914	3·02	18·90	7·60	3·59	33·11	40·2	12·10	8	3861	3299
1322	1915	3·60	9·46	17·07	4·26	34·39	39·7	20·37	10	3356	3065
1323	1916	9·38	7·75	8·55	9·84	35·52	28·2	0·55	13	5526	1700
1324	1917	15·63	13·80	4·36	7·33	41·12	22·1	11·59	11	1330	881
1325	1918	20·08	10·98	22·33	2·15	55·49	43·4	15·05	6	2230	1824
1326	1919	5·72	6·18	6·32	2·95	21·17	51·6	38·56	9	2617	2196
1327	1920	4·00	9·85	7·74	6·43	28·02	38·9	16·1	12	1864	1516
1328	1921	5·94	10·87	10·15	4·56	31·52	32·3	5·0	8	1655	1340
1329	1922	12·80	7·10	—	5·91	25·81	21·7	8·9	8	1177	841
1330	1923	6·68	9·27	8·02	8·37	32·34	21·9	10·2	3	1140	928
1331	1924	5·89	9·51	10·74	10·51	36·65	21·9	8·9	9	1356	1009
1332	1925	5·07	9·44	7·94	—	22·45	18·8	18·8	9	1399	1054
1333	1926	5·72	14·50	13·39	7·12	40·73	28·2	12·6	6	1725	1448
1334	1927	7·48	13·56	6·98	5·20	33·17	21·8	7·5	6	1671	1375
1335	1928	—	15·29	7·16	1·83	24·33	21·9	7·9	10	—	—
1336	1929	9·00	13·51	7·27	3·50	33·28	19·6	16·0	15	—	—

CORRELATION WITH RAINFALL AND HEALTH.

As the general fertility of the soil in the plots under review does not appear to have changed appreciably during the last 38 years, the large fluctuations in the yield of paddy from year to year must have been caused by other factors.

The causes might be many, for in the practice of farming there are innumerable factors which exert an appreciable influence. The quality of seed, the quantity of tillage, the amount of moisture available at different times, the range of temperature, the effects of cloud, the damage from insects and crop diseases and so on all affect the yield. Indeed the factors that are likely to bring about variations are too many to be mentioned. All that we can do is to select certain factors regarding which information is available, and the relation of which to the annual average of yield per bigha (Table 1, column 17) can be measured.

Table given the actually observed correlations of the yield with 12 different factors. The coefficients of correlation were all worked out by the product moment formula from data given in Table 5.

TABLE 6. CORRELATION WITH YIELD PER BIGHA OF PADDY (1894-1932).

Variate	Number of years (n)	Coefficient of correlation
RAINFALL IN BOLPUR STATION		
1. June	34	+0·2614
2. July	36	+0·2292
3 August	35	+0·0807
4. September	35	+0·0932
5. Total Seasonal (June—September) rainfall ...	36	+0·1645
EXCESS OF BIRTHS OVER DEATHS (BIRBHUM DISTRICT)		
6. Year previous to crop season	36	+0·2000
7. Same year as crop season	36	+0·2800
8. Year succeeding crop season	36	+0·1900
NUMBER OF DEATHS		
9. Total deaths in Bahadurpur	27	+0·0465
10. Total deaths in Bolpur Thana	24	−0·2309
11. Fever deaths in Birbhum District	36	−0·2879
12. Fever deaths in Bolpur Thana	24	−0·3705

The 5% value of the coefficient of correlation is found from R. A. Fisher's Table V (Statistical Methods for Research Workers, pp. 224-5) to be 0·3809 for $n=25$. It will be noticed therefore that practically all the correlations are negligible. Only one correlation appears to be on verge of significance ; the total number of fever deaths in Bolpur Thana ($r=-0{\cdot}37$) may have some connexion with the per bigha yield of paddy in Bahadurpur.*

*Even this I think is doubtful in view of the fact that the correlation of $-0{\cdot}37$ is the largest in magnitude in a batch of 12 observed coefficients.

Let r_m be the largest of n observed coefficients of correlation, and p the probability of obtaining a coefficient of correlation which is equal to or greater than r_m. Then $(1-p)$ is the probability that an observel coefficient of correlation will be less than r_m, and $(1-p)^n$ the probability than n observed correlation coefficients will be less than r_m. If we work with a 5 per cent. level of significance, we must put $(1-p)^n = 1-{\cdot}05 = 0{\cdot}95$. For $n=12$, we get $p={\cdot}00427$. From *Tables for Statisticians and Biometricians*, Part II (Edited by Karl Pearson), Table XXXII, p. 206 we find that for a size of sample $=24$, and $p={\cdot}004$, the value of $r_m=0{\cdot}54$. The largest of 12 observed coefficients of correlation should therefore be equal to or exceed 0·54 in order to reach the 5% level of significance.

—*P. C. Mahalanobis.*

Of course we can surmise that there is some relation between health and agriculture, but this relation can only be indirect and partial. And here is another interesting point: the correlation between the number of total deaths in Bolpur Thana and the average yield is only +0·25 which being below the 5% level of significance is negligible; whereas, it is the correlation between *deaths from fever* in Bolpur Thana and the average yield that seems to have some significance. In other words, it is not how many people die, but rather how many people die of fever that seems to matter in connexion with local agricultrue. And this is plausible too, for, death in itself, unless it is extremely widespread, is not likely to affect agriculture. An epidemic of cholera or smallpox carries away a large number of people in a few weeks, but, that cannot generally be expected to affect the average yield of land. What would affect the average yield, however, would be prolonged illness of a large proportion of the population continuing throughout the cultivation season; for this would tell upon the intensity of care and cultivation bestowed upon the crop. And this is exactly what the number of deaths from fever stands for. When many have died of fever in a particular year, we know that many more must have suffered over a long period; and agriculture must have suffered also.

Some people have before now tried to establish this correlation between malaria and agriculture. Dr. Bentley, the erstwhile Director of Public Health of Bengal, was the foremost worker in this line. In his book on Malaria and Agriculture in Bengal (1925), he has given many instances where a relation between the increase of malaria and the deterioration of agriculture is quite evident. For example, he has shown the connexion between the increase of population and the decrease of fallow land in the Dacca Division where there is no fever, and along with it he has shown how in the Burdwan Division where there is excessive malaria, the fallow lands have increased and so on. Our study, therefore, only adds to what Dr. Bentley has shown.

SUMMARY.

Yields of paddy and straw for 38 years (1894-1931) were collected for a single group of plots in Bahadurpur village (in Lower Birbhum, Bengal) from the family records of a local land-owner. A detailed analysis of the data showed:—

(1) The average yield was 5·40 mds. per bigha (1344 lbs. per acre).

(2) The average yield of plots cultivated under the direct supervision of the owner was 6·52 mds. per bigha (1623 lbs. per acre), and 4·27 mds. per bigha (1063 lbs. per acre) for plots cultivated on the share system. It appears therefore that either the land given out to tenants is generally less fertile, or the tenants are usually too poor to cultivate the land adequately; possibly both factors are in operation.

(3) There were large fluctuations in yield from year to year, but the trend-line was practically horizontal showing that the average fertility of the land had remained practically steady during 37 years.

(4) There were also large variations in the area under cultivation, but there was a general upward tendency.

(5) Land under direct cultivation showed a fairly steady rise, but land given out on the share system showed very heavy fluctuations. The rise in the case of land under direct cultivation was probably associated with the steady rise in prices, because when the price of paddy is rising it is more profitable for the owner to pay the labourers in cash.

(6) Correlational analysis did not reveal any significant influence of rainfall and various other factors on the yield per bigha.

(7) The correlation between yield per bigha and the number of fever deaths in the Bolpur Thana was $-0{\cdot}37$ (for $n=24$ years) and was possibly just significant. When many people have died of fever in a particular year we know that many more must have suffered from fever for a long time. This would withdraw many workers from the field and thus exert a harmful effect on production. The connexion between fever deaths and yield is therefore quite plausible.

(*Received December, 1933*).

EDITORIAL NOTE

It will be seen from Table 1 that the size and number of plots as well as the total area for which records are available are fluctuating considerably from year to year. For any particular year we can obtain the 'average yield' either by dividing the total yield by the total acreage (given in Table 1), or from the frequency distributions of yield (given in Table 3) ; the two values will in general be different, since the size of the plots is not constant. From either set of average yields for particular years we can then find the trend (*a*) by giving the same weight to the averages, or (*b*) by giving different weights (according to the total area, or the total number of plots as the case may be). We shall therefore obtain four distinct solutions corresponding to :—

(1) Averages based on total areas without weighting.

(2) Averages based on total areas with weighting.

(3) Averages based on frequency distribution without weighting.

(4) Averages based on frequency distribution with weighting.

The significance of each of the above solutions will naturally be different. Let us consider the chief factors which cause variations in the yield.

(*a*) The climatic factors and conditions of cultivation change from year to year and cause variations in the yield even in the same plot.

(*b*) The fertility of the soil varies from plot to plot, so that the yields are different in different plots even in the same year.

(*c*) Records of yield in any particular year are not available for the whole but only for a portion of the total area under cultivation in the village, and as this portion varies from year to year (not necessarily in a random manner), certain further fluctuations are imposed on the estimates of the yield.

(*d*) We also have the errors of measurement, and finally the random fluctuations due to a variety of small causes.

If the primary data had been presented in complete detail with the size and yield of each plot in each year, we could make an attempt to assess directly the relative importance of the different factors of variation. Unfortunately the condensed form of the data renders this impossible, and we are obliged to have recourse to certain general considerations.

TABLE N 1. YIELDS OF RICE IN MAUNDS PER BIGHA.

No.	Estimate of Yield based on	Weights	Yield in maunds per bigha			Standard deviation in maunds per bigha		
			Owner-cultivated	Share-system	Total	Owner-cultivated	Share	Total
(1)	Total area ...	Unweighted	6·40 ± ·26	4·37 ± ·18	5·58 ± ·22	2·40 ± ·19	1·68 ± ·13	2·01 ± ·16
(2)	Total area ...	Weighted	6·52 ± ·30	4·27 ± ·17	5·40 ± ·19	2·74 ± ·21	1·53 ± ·12	1·76 ± ·14
(3)	Number of plots ...	Unweighted	7·32 ± ·05	5·34 ± ·04	6·56 ± ·03	2·14 ± ·03	1·30 ± ·03	1·82 ± ·02
(4)	Number of plots ...	Weighted	7·74 ± ·07	5·22 ± ·07	6·79 ± ·05	3·00 ± ·04	2·43 ± ·05	3·05 ± ·04

TABLE N 2. YIELDS OF RICE IN LBS. PER ACRE.

No.	Estimate of Yield based on	Weights	Yield in lb per Acre			Standard deviation in lb per acre		
			Owner-cultivated	Share system	Total	Owner-cultivated	Share	Total
(1)	Total area ...	Unweighted ...	1598 ± 65	1088 ± 46	1389 ± 55	597 ± 46	418 ± 32	500 ± 39
(2)	Total area ...	Weighted ...	1623 ± 75	1063 ± 42	1344 ± 48	682 ± 53	381 ± 29	438 ± 34
(3)	Number of plots ...	Unweighted ...	1822 ± 12	1329 ± 10	1633 ± 7	533 ± 7	324 ± 7	453 ± 5
(4)	Number of plots ...	Weighted ...	1927 ± 17	1299 ± 17	1690 ± 12	747 ± 10	605 ± 12	759 ± 10

It will be easily seen that the number of plots will control factor (*d*), but in the absence of any assurance that the plots constitute a random sample it is doubtful how much value can be attached to mere replication. In fact, in case the samples are not random, weighting by the number of plots is likely to make the estimates of average yield.

The total area for which records are available on the other hand will control factors (*b*) and (*c*). When the total area for which records are available is large it will include soils of different grades and will thus give a reliable estimate of the average yield ; on the other hand, when the total area is small the estimate may not be fully representative. On this view, weighting according to area would be desirable.

Finally in case the seasonal factor (*a*) is the dominant one (in the sense that fluctuations from year to year are more important than fluctuations from field to field within the same year), then it is clear that it will not matter very much whether we work with the unweighted or the weighted averages.

In view of the interest of the question I am giving the results obtained by different methods for $n=38$ years in Tables N1 and N2 (p. 16).

Fitting a straight line by the direct correlation method we find the following constants.

TABLE N (3)

	Method of calculation	"Weights"	r=Coefficient of correlation	b=Coefficient of Regression	Ratio of Owner : Share
1	Total Area ...	Unweighted ..	−0·0087	−0·0016	1·46
2	Total Area	Weighted ...	−0·0098	−0·0016	1·58
3	Number of Plots	Unweighted ..	−0·0068	−0·0446	1·37
4	Number of Plots	Weighted ...	−0·0319	−0·0047	1·48

Several things are clear from the above results :—

(*i*) The ratio of the yield for Owner-cultivated to the yield under the Share-system comes out substantially the same (about 1.5) in all cases.

(*ii*) The results for 'weighted' and 'unweighted' averages are in close agreement. This suggests that the seasonal changes are probably the most important causes of variations in the yield.

(*iii*) The coefficients of correlation and regression are negligibly small in all cases.

We may therefore conclude that there has not occurred any appreciable change in the soil-fertility so that the average yield has on the whole remained practically the same during the period under review. The yield under Owner-cultivation has however been about 50 per cent. higher than the yield under the Share-system.

As regards actual estimates I think on the whole it will be preferable to adopt the weighted averages based on total areas which give the following trend equation :—

$$y = 5{\cdot}40 - 0{\cdot}0016\ (t - 1913)$$

where y=yield of paddy in maunds per bigha and t=year.

—*P. C. Mahalanobis.*

APPENDIX.—Sample of Records kept By Mr. Jagatbandhu Pal for the Paddy Yields of his Lands in Bahadurpur Village in Birbhum District in Bengal —*Bengali era 1309 (1902 A. D.)*

A.—Pertaining to lands cultivated under his own supervision.

Date	Area			Description of Plot	No. of Units	Total Measurement of Unit					
	B.	K.	Ch.			Sr.	Ch.	Mp.	Sl.	Sr.	Ch.
6 Kartic	0	8	0	Koler Math, Aus	17	12	0	1	2	4	0
12 ,,	0	11	0	Koler Math, Aus just below the big pond ...	20	12	0	1	4	0	0
3 Agrahayan	0	11	0	,, ,, bought from Gour Surya ...	25	12	0	1	7	0	0
8 ,,	0	14	0	Ajars Field. Bakuri (Big plot)	18	12	0	1	2	16	0
5 Magh	2	17	0	Majumdar's Kori, Ishan's Kori and Ghosal's Devottar	67	11	5	4	5	17	4

B.—Pertaining to lands cultivated on share basis.

Date	Area			Description of Plot	No. of Units	Total Measurement of Unit					Share of Labour				Owner's Share			
	B.	K.	Ch.			Sr.	Mp.	Sl.	Sr.	Ch.	Mp.	Sl.	Sr.	C.	Mp.	Sl.	Sr.	C.
13 Agrahayan	0	8	0	Ajar's field. Upper section Katke grown. Sharer Duk Bayen	11	12	0	6	12	0	0	3	6	0	0	3	6	0
19 Pous	3	0	3	Bakuri to the south of Ajar. Sharer Makhar Kot	90	9	0	5	0	10	2	2	4	8	2	6	5	0

C.—Pertaining to records of annual yield of straw.

Description of Land	Area	1309
	B. K. Ch.	
East field, South of the Kalu's Plot	0 8 0	3—18
Plot north of the above	0 4 0	1— 5
Ajar Field Bakuri	0 14 0	4—17
Sethor Field. Ghosal's Bakuri	2 2 10	1-1-16

Appendix III

Sample of Handbills Used for Sensitizing the Villagers

প্রচারপত্র—১৯

ম্যালেরিয়ার প্রতিকার

ম্যালেরিয়ার কারণ—

মশার কামড়ে ম্যালেরিয়া হয়ঃ—

মশার জন্ম—

ডোবার জলে ও ঘরের আনাচে-কানাচে যে সকল ভাঙ্গা হাঁড়ি বা টিনের কানেস্তারা থাকে তাহাতে জল জমিয়া প্রচুর মশা হয়; মশা দিনের বেলায় ঝোপ-জঙ্গলে আশ্রয় নেয় ও সন্ধ্যাবেলা নিকটস্থ গৃহস্থের ঘরে প্রবেশ করে।

(ক) **মশা জন্মিতে দিবে নাঃ—**

(১) অনাবশ্যক ডোবা বুজাইয়া ফেলিবে এবং ঝোপ-জঙ্গল পরিষ্কার করিবে।

(২) পুষ্করিণীর **আগাছা পরিষ্কার** করিবে।

(৩) গ্রামের জল বাহির করিবার জন্য ভাল করিয়া **ড্রেন কাটিবে,** এবং প্রত্যেক বাড়ির সহিত সেই ড্রেনের যোগ করিয়া দিবে; তাহা হইলে কোথাও জল জমিতে পারিবে না।

(৪) যে সকল ডোবা বুজাইয়া দেওয়া সম্ভবপর নহে সে গুলিতে **সপ্তাহে একদিন কেরোসিন দিবে;** তাহা হইলে মশা জন্মিতে পারিবে না।

(৫) কৈ, খলিশা, তেচোকো মাছ মশার বাচ্চা খায়; সেই সকল **মাছ পুকুরে ছাড়িয়া দিবে।**

(৬) মশারীর ভিতর শয়ন করিবে।

(৭) সন্ধ্যাবেলা ঘরে ধূপ-ধুনা দিবে।

(খ) **ভাল চিকিৎসা করাইবেঃ—**

(১) যাহাদের প্লীহা বড়ো, তাহারা উপযুক্ত চিকিৎসকের নিকট ঔষধপত্রের ব্যবস্থা করিবে।

যাহাদের গ্রামে চিকিৎসক নাই, তাহারা শ্রীনিকেতনে খবর দিলে, আমরা সাধ্যমত চিকিৎসার ব্যবস্থা করিব।

পল্লী সেবা বিভাগ।

শ্রীনিকেতন, বিশ্বভারতী।

Appendix IV

Varieties of Signature Handicraft Made in Sriniketan

VISVA-BHARATI

CATALOGUE

OF

SRINIKETAN HANDICRAFTS

1933-34

Asans and Durries

Asans – 2′ x 3′
Rs. 1-12 each

Durry – 6′ x 8′
Rs. 25 each

Weaving

Saree
Rs. 1-12 per piece

Table Cloth
Rs. 1-8 each

Batik and Embroidery

Batik—Silk Blouse Piece
Rs. 5 each

Embroidered pelmets for windows and doors
Rs. 25 each

Batik—Cotton Table Cloth
Rs. 4-8 each

Embroidered Silk Chaddar
Rs. 30 each

Leather Work

Leather Bag—Rs. 7-8 each

Ladies' Hand Bag—Rs. 3-4 each

Embroidered Leather Cushions—Rs. 10 each

Book Binding

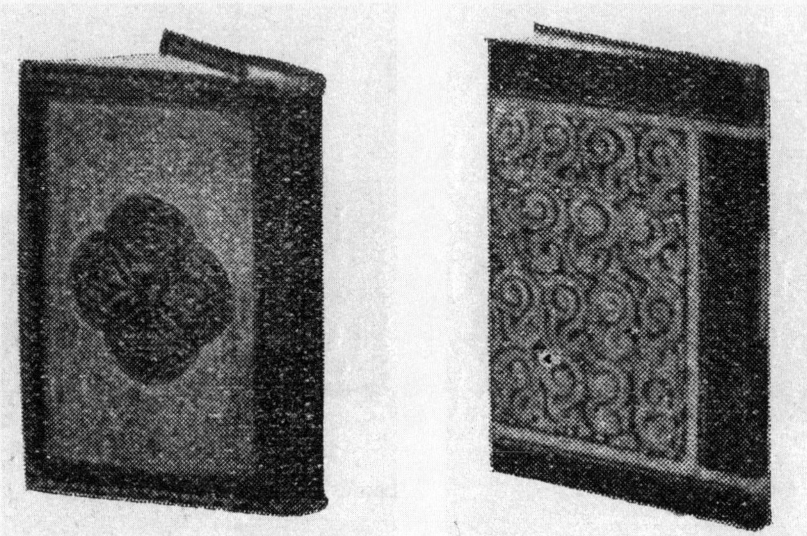

Autograph photo albums and book covers
From Re. 1 to Rs. 10

Lacquer Work

Various useful and ornamental articles
From As. 2 to Rs. 20

Acknowledgements

I would like to gratefully acknowledge the help I have received from the archives and the libraries where I have carried out this research over long years on the history of rural reconstruction at Santiniketan's twin campus in Sriniketan. My main source has been the Rabindra-Bhavana Archives, its library, its museum, and its audio-visual and reprography unit. At Rabindra-Bhavana, I would like to especially mention Professor Amal Pal, Director, Rabindra-Bhavana, Shri Nilanjan Bandopadhyay, Officer on Special Duty, Dr Pradip Mandal, Curator, Shri Shovan Ruj of the Bhavana's archives, Shri Utpal Mitra, formerly of the Bhavana's archives, Shri Sourav Chakraborty, and Sm. Saswati Karmakar of the audio-visual and reprography unit. and Dr Sabahat Nausheen, Sm. Seema Hazra, Shri Mafijul Islam of Rabindra-Bhavana's library.

I would be failing in my duty if I did not mention a former librarian of Rabindra-Bhavana, Sm. Supriya Ray, who helped me to track down some of the Sriniketan pioneers. Supriya's grandfather-in-law, Kimtaro Kasahara, and father-in-law, Dhirananda Roy, were among the leading Sriniketan pioneers.

I have also used with great benefit the 'Leonard Elmhirst Papers' in the Dartington Hall Trust Archive, United Kingdom. There I would like to remember the wonderful personality of Peter Cox, Founder-Principal of the Dartington College of Arts, who worked closely with Dartington Trust's founders, Leonard and Dorothy Elmhirst. Remarkably, while writing my humble tribute, I realize that Peter Cox died on 13 April 2015, aged 97.

Visuals of Sriniketan from the Rabindra-Bhavana Archive Collection

L.K. Elmhirst at Sriniketan, 1922–23

L.K. Elmhirst at Sriniketan, 1922–23

Young Dorothy Elmhirst

Dorothy Elmhirst

Sriniketan community with Rabindranath at 'Cheap Kuthi'

Prime Minister Nehru at Sriniketan, 1952

Mahatma Gandhi at Sriniketan, 1941, in front of the Halakarshana mural by Nandalal Bose in Cheap Kuthi

Rabindranath Tagore and L.K. Elmhirst

Kuala tree house built by Japanese gardener, Kasahara, 1923

Boy learning a craft at Sriniketan

Sriniketan landscape

Boys playing tug of war on Sports Day at Sriniketan

Sriniketan Experimental Farm

Brati-Balaka boys doing drill at Sriniketan

Girls' class at Sriniketan with teacher Indu Sudha Ghosh

Sriniketan community with Rabindranath, 1936; among others are Nandalal Bose, Santosh Bhanja, Sudhindra Chandra Ray and Tarak Dhar

Trainees painting *alpana* at Sriniketan

Science class with Gourgopal Ghosh

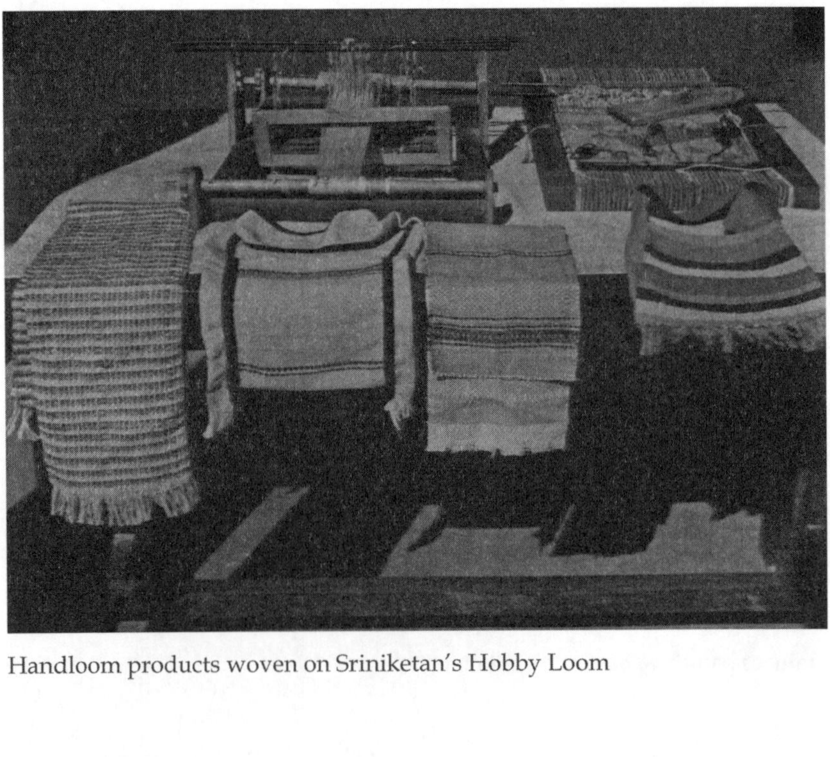

Handloom products woven on Sriniketan's Hobby Loom

Bookbinding class at Sriniketan

Sriniketan community with L.K. Elmhirst, Kalimohan Ghosh and Gourgopal Ghosh among others, 1923

Artisans and trainees working on Sriniketan's power looms, 1936

Mahatma Gandhi at Sriniketan, 1941

Ruins around Sriniketan

Lac workers at Sriniketan

Making clay pottery at Sriniketan

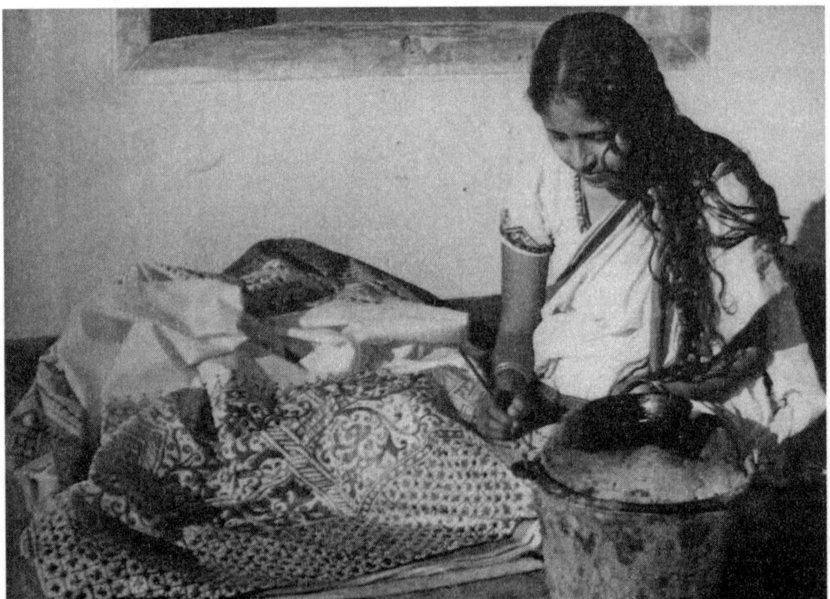

Batik work at Sriniketan

Clay pottery store room at Sriniketan

Leather craft at Sriniketan

Learning to work the power loom

Crafting an outdoor decoration at Sriniketan

Sanitation class at Sriniketan with health worker Nanibala Roy

Village boys in Siksha-Satra class

Siksha-Satra open-air class

Library, Sriniketan Institute of Rural Reconstruction

Irrigation pump used by Sriniketan farmers

Sriniketan community with Nurse Gretchen Green, 1920s

Sriniketan students working in the fields

Sriniketan students raising a garden

Co-educational class at Sriniketan

Rabindranath conducting Sriniketan's Halakarshana ceremony

Power loom at work in Sriniketan

Baul singers at Sriniketan Mela

Sriniketan Kuthi Bari or 'Cheap Kuthi' as named after John Cheap